D1304500

DISCARDED

# SOLID LIVING
## in a
# SHATTERED WORLD

# WILLIAM H. HINSON

Abingdon Press
Nashville

SOLID LIVING IN A SHATTERED WORLD

This book is printed on acid-free paper.

**Library of Congress Cataloging in Publication Data**

HINSON, WILLIAM H., 1936-
  Solid living in a shattered world.
   1. Methodist Church—Sermons. 2. United Methodist Church
(U.S.)—Sermons. 3. Sermons, American. I. Title.
BX8333.H555S65     1985      252'.076      84-27993

**ISBN 0-687-39048-6**

MANUFACTURED BY THE PARTHENON PRESS AT
NASHVILLE, TENNESSEE, UNITED STATES OF AMERICA

*To my wife, Jean,*
*whose unselfish love*
*and constant encouragement*
*put steadiness in the steps*
*of all her family*

## Acknowledgments

The material contained in this volume was originally delivered to Abingdon Press to be published in non-sermonic form for inquiring laypersons. When the South Central Jurisdiction Communications Committee informed me that I had been chosen as the United Methodist representative on the 1985 series of the Protestant Hour, the content of the book was once more arranged into sermons.

Preparing these messages and recording them for The Protestant Hour has been an enriching experience for me. The producer of the United Methodist series, David Abernathy, is a seminary classmate of mine. His personal courage, together with his incredible knowledge of the skills required in the religious communication field, have increased my admiration for his life and ministry.

Bill Horlock, also a seminary classmate, and his cooperative staff made my working days in Atlanta a joyful reunion. My understanding and appreciation for quality religious broadcasts have been increased by the competent workers at the Protestant Radio and Television Center.

To be given the opportunity to preach the Gospel to millions of persons through hundreds of radio stations across the earth is every preacher's highest aspiration. I am grateful to those who gave me this high privilege.

My thanks to Gail Keller, my secretary, for typing and retyping the manuscript and encouraging me along the way.

The leaders and staff of First Church, Houston, help the pastor guard his morning hours for reading, studying, and writing. Without their thoughtfulness, this book could not have been written.

Most of all I am grateful to my wife, Jean, and to my children, Beth, John, and Cathy. They are my companions in ministry. Through their own deep commitments and supportive understanding, they set me free to serve and make me feel good about serving.

# Contents

Preface..................................................7
Introduction............................................. 9
I SOLID LIVING IN A SHATTERED WORLD
  *Beginning with God's Love*............................11
II IRON WITH THE HOTTEST IRON
  *One Day at a Time*.................................... 21
III OUR MISLAID LORD
  *Looking for Christ*.................................... 31
IV OUR GOD—THE LAST OF THE
  BIG SPENDERS
  *Your Heart Can Experience God's Presence*....... 40
V GOD'S MYSTERIOUS GIFT
  *How Can I Find Forgiveness?*......................... 52
VI SOMETIMES HE KNOCKS WITH
  BLOODY KNUCKLES
  *Opening Up to God*.................................... 64
VII WHEN FAITH GROWS COLD
  *Four Steps Toward Renewing Your Faith*........... 75
VIII THE ROOTS OF OUR JOY
  *Entering into Joy*.................................... 88
IX JUST A BUNCH OF BUILDERS
  *From Hindrance to Helper*............................99
X WHEN WILL THE WORLD BELIEVE?
  *Someone Has to Make It Real*....................... 111
XI HOPE CAN HELP
  *Overcoming Discouragement*......................... 124
XII THE PRAYER OF POWER
  *The Practice of Prayer*.............................. 134
XIII THE GOD WHO LEADS ALSO PRECEDES
  *He Is Going Before You*............................. 145
Conclusion............................................. 157

# Preface

This book was written to help people see God at work in their world. God's activity did not end with the last page of the Bible. The eternal principles and lessons within the Scriptures are spelled out daily in our demanding, modern world. These chapters are written to help people connect the God of the Bible with the one who is powerfully present in the everyday events that shape and define their lives.

God accomplishes the extraordinary, but he works through the ordinary. The stories and sermons of Jesus are profound in terms of the weighty truth they convey. They are, however, framed in images that were familiar to all persons. For Jesus, earth was "crammed with heaven" (Elizabeth Barrett Browning, "Aurora Leigh"). He saw God at work in the wild flowers, the birds, the crops in the fields, in the farmer who plowed his land, and in all people—rich, poor, rural, urban. In all of them Jesus saw something he related to God. He saw the supernatural in the natural.

When our lives are overwhelmed with rapid, unbelievable change, when we are unsure about tomorrow, when we feel forsaken, alone, and deeply hurt, we have a desperate need to discover the

presence of God. If we can find him, if we can know
that he is present, we can make it.

I believe the work of God can be seen in the events
around us, in our world. And even in a shattered
world like ours, when faith opens our eyes and ears,
we can see and hear those lessons and helps God has
for us. Seeing and hearing them can put steadiness in
all our steps.

*William H. Hinson*

# Introduction

I have written this book for one basic purpose. This is simply to help you to grow in your relationship with your heavenly Father. You may have often wondered if you could grow closer to God. More than that, however, you may have felt now and then a touch of that special thirst for God's presence. This is the beginning of God's miraculous work that prompts you to open your heart to him.

You will discover in reading this book that I am inviting you to try a fresh walk of faith. This walk will cover several steps that most of us find are helpful in our own walk with Christ. The first step involves the great reality of God's abounding love for us. From this beginning point we discover that God's concern for us enables us to reevaluate our current priorities. It also opens the door of God's grace of forgiveness and then leads us, in turn, to open our lives further to him.

I hope that these opening chapters may serve as a special means of preparation for you. They are intended to lead you into the next section, the place in this journey of faith where I share with you my deep personal conviction that the living Christ wants to enter into your life and to become your friend. I am very excited about this for I believe that Christ offers us a life that is magnificent in many ways. He deals with our insensitivity to his ways and helps us to open our hearts to his love. This often kindles a profound sense of vitality and warmth, renewing our faith and our understanding. With a few very specific suggestions from the experiences of others on this path of faith, your awareness of God's presence can grow clearer and more compelling.

As you continue on this path, you will feel a growing interest in people around you. Reaching out to help them, building them up and encouraging them, your spiritual experience will grow deeper. You may even find that before long you are helping others to become aware of the reality of Christ in a more meaningful way.

In the closing chapters of the book I will try to help you with several prevalent concerns. One is the widespread problem of discouragement. The second is the need for prayer. And the last is a conviction that God will be with you as you face the future. Through all of those chapters I have shared some of the ways in which I believe you can live solid, stable lives, even in a shattered world.

# I

# Solid Living
# in a Shattered World

*Beginning with God's Love*

The last child had gone to college, and the family pet had died. Susan had majored in motherhood for thirty years, and now her nest was empty. The many tasks she had done for her family, and in which she had defined her being, were no longer required. Even more shattering, her husband left her for a younger woman and asked for a divorce. Susan suddenly found herself unneeded by her children, unwanted by her husband, and alone. Her world had come apart. Now she had to find a new place to live, a job outside the home, and a new life for herself.

Susan's world was completely shaken up. There are many Susans today. As you are reading this you could be saying to yourself, "I've also gone through things that have shaken my world apart." In one way or another, Susan's experience has become nearly a universal experience. Our whole world seems to be shaken apart. It's not just ourselves as individuals. What makes it all so confusing is that we see the same kinds of things going on in the world around us.

Morally, we seem to have lost our moorings. Human life, as in the days of old Rome when babies were left abandoned in the alleys and streets, has become cheap again. Here in Houston and other

American cities, we see the same thing occurring again and again as babies are abandoned in trash bins. We feel pressure from many to grow more like our culture, to relax our standards, and to accept that which is foreign to the way we were brought up. Some would have us simply shrug our shoulders and say, "Oh well, times change, and we have to change with them." I read the other day an advice columnist who's read by millions. She received a letter from a young man who wrote, "I'm thirty, I've never been married; I've never had an affair; do you think I'm normal?" This lady wrote him back, saying, "Probably not." And I thought, here is someone who is supposed to be a bastion of middle-class morality telling this young man who is struggling to hold on to some standards perhaps acquired in Sunday school that he is probably not normal.

Economically, ours is a shook-up world. Someone declared the other day, "I now pay more money in taxes than I made fifteen years ago, and I'm not sure I can make ends meet." And who can forget the story we've all heard about the Federal Savings and Loan man who, when someone asked, "How are you weathering the increase in interest rates again?" declared, "Why I'm making it all right; I sleep like a baby. Every hour I wake up and cry a little bit!"

This is no joke. Most of us simply see no way that we can ever be financially secure. In fact, if your savings are only the equivalent of one or two months expenses, you are like most people around you.

In the realm of global uneasiness, it's a field day for speculation. Not long ago I had a chance to go to St. Mary's, Georgia, to see the submarine base there. I had the additional privilege of touring one of the nuclear subs in port at the time. I went down into that thing. I don't know how people live in it. The commander took me past sixteen missiles all set, ready to be fired from deep down in the sea. And then he showed me the red telephone he stays near practically every hour of day and night. I said, "What do you do when you leave here? Where do you go?" He said, "Well, I can't tell you that, but I can tell you that we go out into the oceans of the world. We go deep down into the sea, shut off our engines and hide. I wait beside the phone and hide." I said, "They're hiding, too, aren't they?" And he said, "Of course they are. It's one great hide-and-seek with these submarines as we wait to see whether or not we press the button that starts the third world war."

Where can you acquire the confidence that will allow you to live, not just cope, but to live victoriously even in the middle of circumstances like ours? There was a belief in the Jewish faith that held that when things were perfect between God and his creation, people could go in and out and have absolute security. When Jesus began to describe his own ministry, he chose the image of the good shepherd, saying, "I am the door; if any one enters by me, he will be saved, and will go in and out and find pasture" (John 10:9, RSV). In other words, right in the middle of this shook-up world you can find security in him. That's a promise I hope will become quite real and personal to you soon.

How does the promise come? First of all, he declared, "The sheep hear his voice, and he calls his own sheep by name" (John 10:3, RSV). This image became alive for me when I visited Israel and saw the shepherds with their sheep. They can call the names, the individual names, of all of their sheep. Yet, the sheep all look alike to us! As the flock approaches

13

a well, the shepherd calls their names and obediently, one after the other, they step forward to take their places in the line and get a drink. And then the shepherd goes into the village fold, which may have fifty flocks, thousands of sheep, and walks in and out among the sleeping animals before daylight, whispering the names of his sheep. They silently rise to their feet, follow him out of that fold, and the rest of the sheep don't even hear him!

Jesus says, "I am the good shepherd; I know my own . . ." (John 10:14, RSV). Now what's he saying? He's saying that he is intimately acquainted with our life situation. He knows everything that touches us and hurts us. He knows all of the burdens we bear. He understands our problems. He knows about the conflict within that makes us feel as though we are coming apart when we aren't sure who we are any more. He understands these things. We have someone in Christ who knows. Therefore, nothing is hopeless. We can continue because someone understands. Often we all forget that.

I forgot this promise during my graduate school days at Emory. It was during winter quarter. I'll always remember that afternoon when self-pity simply swallowed me up. I had been to the library and was on my way back to my room. It was a basement room that I called my hole in the ground. I was renting it during the week and then flying home to Savannah on weekends to preach at my church and to be with my family for a few hours. I had been doing that a long time. That dreary day when I was walking to my room, seeing the daddies getting in from work and sharing that wonderful joy of meeting the family, I decided I couldn't take any more. Something snapped inside my soul, and I hurried to my room, pulled out my suitcase from beneath the bed, started throwing my things into it—all the while mentally composing the note I was going to write to my major professor.

I was about to leave the university when I remembered a line I had read only that morning in my devotional. It was a line from Oswald Chambers' book, *My Utmost for His Highest.* He said, "If Jesus ever gave us a command he could not enable us to fulfill, He would be a liar; and . . . it means we are telling God there is something He has not taken into account." And when the truth of that hit me squarely, I knew I could never say that, because if Jesus showed us anything at all about God, he showed us that our God knows everything about us. He has numbered the hairs on our heads. He sees when the tiniest sparrow falls to the earth. This God knows everything that weighs us down and presses us to the earth. And with the realization that he understood, a glorious, wonderful peace came into my soul. Although I have been lonely many times since that day, I have never felt quite as lonely or as forsaken as I did in the moment preceding that gift of peace. Somebody understands. Paul Tournier, the great psychiatrist, said that if we don't have someone who understands us, we become ill. In Christ, we have someone who understands.

The Apostle Paul told about his conversion experience over and over again. One of the things he said was most enlightening to me. Paul described how Christ first spoke to him, saying, "Saul, Saul" in Hebrew. Paul didn't hear Jesus in the Greek tongue, although Paul readily spoke as well as wrote in Greek. Nor did he hear him speaking in Aramaic, though Paul understood Aramaic. Paul said that when Jesus first called his name, "Saul," he did so in the Hebrew tongue. Now Paul knew these other languages, but when he dreamed, probably he dreamed in Hebrew. He perhaps even counted in Hebrew. It was the revered tongue of his heritage. What this suggests to me is that when God comes to people, he always comes in the most intimate, the most personal way imaginable, because he knows all about us. Nothing then is hopeless. If your world has become badly shaken, remember this—God really understands. We can hang on a little longer because someone knows.

And then, marvelously, not only does he know all about us, this Scripture says, but he accepts and loves us. "The good shepherd lays down his life for the sheep" (John 10:11, RSV). In spite of the fact that he knows all of our secrets and all that we try to cover up, he still lays down his life for us. Ultimately, that is what makes the difference, isn't it?

That's what made the difference for me. If God had fought with me on my own terms, I think I never would have surrendered to him. But all the while I was struggling with whether or not to become a Christian, whether to be a minister, trying to shut God out, he never shut me out. I stopped saying my prayers; I stopped reading my Bible. I would not let myself even think about God. I would have stopped going to church, but you couldn't do that and live with Mother. If you didn't go to church, Mother counted the silverware! She didn't trust anyone who didn't go to church. But, while I had to go to church, nobody could make me listen. When the preacher started talking, I'd glaze my eyes and walk about in my mind. I created a life of fantasy in order to avoid God.

Finally, in my desperate attempt to elude God, I was reduced to the ridiculous posture of going down in the woods in back of our house and shouting to the stumps. I would say, "Damn you, God, stop interfering with my life." And every time I said something as ridiculous as that, I could hear, like an echo, a small voice inside my soul saying, "But, Bill, I love you, and I want you to be my man." And finally, one day I couldn't fight that anymore. I came to the conclusion that if he could love me, in spite of all that I was and all that I was not, then the least I could do was spend the rest of my life serving him—that was the least I could give.

The good news of the gospel is that God loves us even when we aren't lovable. The Good Shepherd knows all about us and still lays down his life for us. His unconditional love is called grace. Grace is what can make the difference for you.

Grace is what saved Simon Peter. Do you remember the time that Peter denied knowing Jesus? If Jesus had denounced Peter, told him how ungrateful and insensitive he was, Peter would have clenched his jaw, stridden out of Caiaphas's courtyard and never looked back. However, when Peter heard that soft step behind him and knew that Jesus had heard his denial, he surely turned and looked into a face rent with disappointment, somehow still full of love. It was that unconditional love that led Peter to repentance and stability.

The story of the woman at the well in Samaria also illustrates the power of this love. After Jesus told her about the brokenness in her personal life, she went back to the village. Why do you think the Samaritan woman ran back to the village that ostracized her? It was not just because Jesus confronted her with her immorality. Any pious busybody could have preached to her about all of the men in her life. What really put wings on her feet and gave her a new possibility for living was that Christ did know all about her, and still offered her "living water"! "Come, see a man!" she declared. "He knows all about me and he still loves me!" (John 4:29).

I agree with one who said, "Becoming a Christian is like falling in love." One day you just can't thumb your nose at him anymore. You can't stiff-arm his love anymore. One day you come to the conclusion that you've hurt him enough. You want to cooperate with him now; you want to give your life back to him. He's died for you, and that's the least you can do.

How could he love you like that? Let me tell you how. I met Gus when he was six weeks old. A church member (I don't know whether I have forgiven him yet) brought Gus to our house in a lard can. Gus was a Siamese kitten. Our son was almost two, and because that layman wanted to give him a gift before we moved to Savannah, he brought Gus. The kitten had been so named because he was an ugly kitten and the ugliest man in our town (according to the layman), was a man named Gus. I should have put the lid on the can right then, but I didn't. I took Gus to Savannah in an unairconditioned mini-compact. My family rode in my mother-in-law's comfortable sedan, but I rode in our little car, with Gus yowling all the way on that hot June afternoon. When I reached Savannah, I didn't have a simple headache; I had an extra-strength headache. I wasn't in any shape to meet any parishioners or anybody; I was mainly disgusted with the cat.

It was the beginning of a long and interesting relationship. Gus wouldn't eat normal food; he had to have the most expensive kind. He was always clawing on things. We had to have him declawed. We did all

18

kinds of expensive things for him. I remember how, when Gus wanted water, he would stand in the tub and yowl until you adjusted the water so it could run down his throat. It had to be just right. If it came too fast, he yowled; if it came too slow, he yowled. And, somehow, as though to really finish the chapter, he became seriously ill while I was away at General Conference, and my family had the vet keep him alive through intravenous feedings until I could get back for the funeral. I tell you, when the vet sent me his bill, he sent a sympathy card with it!

My brothers, who knew I was a dog man from the word go, and that I didn't have much love for cats, shook their heads in amazement saying, "Bill, why do you put up with that animal?" What they didn't understand (but should have) was that every night from the time our son was two, until Gus died, John carried that old cat, like a piece of wood, up the stairs to bed. There they put their heads on the same pillow. In the bad times and in the good times, Gus was there for John. And the two of them got linked up together. We had to love Gus for John's sake.

Somehow we need to get hold of that. Our Father doesn't love us because we're good, or even because we're worthy. We may be children of God, but many of us haven't been a real child of God. He loves us so much that he bound us up with Christ! He has a son invested in us. Christ belongs to us, and we belong to Christ. When we come home from the far country with the dirt of the pigpens still on our souls, God loves us and cleanses our lives; he gives us a heart to love him that we didn't have before. He's given a son for us. That's what we celebrate—that's how we can live confidently even in the middle of a shattered world like ours. God wants us to be secure with him forever. Our new future is bound up in the strong love of God for us. It is not determined by anything about ourselves. In fact, our future with God is entirely a free gift.

# II

## Iron with the Hottest Iron

### *One Day at a Time*

Several months ago I was leading a Bible study, and a member of the group shared with us some homespun wisdom she had learned from her housekeeper. It seems this lady had told her housekeeper some of the things that were tearing her apart. Indeed, she confessed, "I feel like I'm falling apart. I'm not a woman. I'm a mob. There are so many of me that I'm going off in all different directions. I'm overextended. I have far too many commitments, too many things out there waiting for me to do." Finally, at the end of her tirade, she said, "I guess I just have too many irons in the fire." And her helper, who had been ironing all the while, and listening to that outpouring of confusion, without so much as looking up, said to her, "Well, then, iron with the one that's hottest!" Iron with the one that's hottest! That's precisely what Jesus said in the sixth chapter of Matthew. The Phillips translation says, "One day's trouble is enough for one day" (6:34). Don't worry about tomorrow's troubles. Another translation declares, "Sufficient unto the day is the evil thereof" (KJV).

This is the next step toward the renewal of faith. For some readers it will be more difficult than for others. However, it is necessary for us all if we are going to grow spiritually. Søren Kierkegaard, the Danish theologian of the nineteenth century, said in *Purity of Heart* that purity of heart is to will one thing. The housekeeper said it in her own way, "Iron with the one that's hottest."

You cannot iron with more than one iron at a time. The skill, the art, is determining which one is hottest. I recognize that that beautiful image of the iron is lost on many people. However some folks can still recall when the irons were placed in front of the fireplace. My grandmother put them all there, and then one after the other she picked them up, and with a moistened fingertip, touched the bottom of the irons to determine which one was ready. It was always delightful to see her go through that little testing ritual to see which one was hottest. And if a child were sick, he was blessed by having one of these hot irons wrapped in a towel and put at the foot of his bed so he could touch his cold feet to it on a winter's night. To determine which iron is hottest is a skill and an art.

I can recall my father trying to teach me how to shoot those South Georgia quail. At first, I tried to shoot down the entire covey. I would empty my gun and never touch a bird. It took my father a long time to explain to me that I had to pick out first one, and then the other, and then the other. Some poor, fragmented people are going through life aiming at the entire covey, forgetting that Jesus says tackle today's trouble. It's sufficient for that day. Somehow, when we take our troubles one day at a time, we divide them. And when we divide our fears, we make them more manageable.

Do you remember Martha's problems? Mary, you'll recall, was sitting at the feet of Jesus. Martha, who was busy in the kitchen being the good hostess, came out to the Master, saying, "Lord, dost thou not care that my sister hath left me to serve alone? bid her therefore that she help me." Our Lord shook his head, saying, "Martha, Martha, thou art careful and troubled about many things" (Luke 10:40-41, KJV). We do indeed get "troubled" when we have so many things coming at us. Oftentimes we simply cannot manage them. We are fragmented, because rather than dealing with life's difficulties one at a time, we're disabled by a preoccupation with tomorrow.

I can believe that old legend about the clock. A huge grandfather clock one day simply stopped ticking, because for the first time it had started trying to add up how many times it would have to tick in its life and it was just too much. We begin to add up all of those things out there tomorrow, and suddenly discover they're too many.

I read once why the animal trainers carry certain objects into the cages. When they're trying to get the lions to sit on the stool or to perform other tricks for the audience, they have a whip in one hand. They also have a pistol strapped to their hip, and that's good insurance! The animal trainers always have the pistol, but I'm told that the most important piece of equipment they carry into the cage is the chair. They hold it by the back and they thrust the legs toward the face of the wild animal. Those who know maintain that the wild animal tries to focus on all four legs at once. In the attempt to focus on all four, a kind of paralysis overwhelms the animal and it becomes tame, weak, and disabled, simply because its attention is fragmented. That story makes a lot of sense to me.

I know that in my own life when I'm trying to think of all kinds of things rather than dealing with one thing at a time, I lose my power. Trying to get all psyched up about something which is not yet is almost like trying to jump a ditch before you get to it. When we think about it rationally, it doesn't make much sense. We can get so preoccupied with the future that the past loses its power.

Do you recall how the disciples were with Jesus one day when he fed the five thousand? They witnessed that tremendous miracle, and shortly afterward Jesus dismissed the crowd and got into the little boat with his disciples to go across to the other side of the Sea of Galilee. While they were on their way across, the disciples started a discussion among themselves. When Jesus spoke to them about the leaven of the Pharisees and Sadducees, they thought he was upset because someone in the group had forgotten to bring bread. Now, they had just come from the feeding of the five thousand! They had seen Jesus take a few fish and some loaves and miraculously multiply it so that all the people had plenty to eat and there were seven basketfuls left over. And yet, only a few minutes away from that miracle, someone in the group turned to another who was supposed to be responsible and said, "Now what are we going to have for supper? You forgot to bring bread." Our Lord must have wrung his hands in despair.

He said to them, "Have you forgotten already? Are your souls like sieves? Are you so preoccupied with what might be tomorrow that you cannot even celebrate today? Does tomorrow and all of its fears and apprehensions have such power, such a hold over you that you cannot, even for a little while, hold on to the inspiration of what God has done in the past?" Well, we say, "That was yesterday, Lord. What are you going to do for me tomorrow?" We forget that the manna was given to the children of

Israel one day at a time. It was fresh every day.

I tell you, the most powerful people in the world are those who can focus. Paul said, "This one thing I do." Jesus, who from the beginning of his ministry saw the cross looming largely before him, could live every day to its fullest, preaching as he walked, and talking to the multitudes. He performed some of his finest and most unforgettable miracles after he knew he was on his way to Jerusalem to die. He was able to focus. He could have been preoccupied with all that he faced, but his directive to, "Seek ye first the kingdom of God," found its finest expression in his life (Matt. 6:33, KJV). Do the things that are nearest at hand. Today's troubles are enough for one day. Don't be anxious about tomorrow. He laid it down then, for all of his followers, saying that we are to live one day at a time.

Why do you think he taught us in the Lord's Prayer to pray, "Give us this day our daily bread?" He didn't say anything about accumulating a reservoir—didn't say anything about having a bank of blessings out there on which we could draw at any time we need them. He said, "Give us each day, this day, our daily bread." I like that rhyme which says, "Life is hard by the yard, but a cinch by the inch." I believe that. Taken in little chunks, we can manage our fears. Thank God; he serves us life one block at a time—only twenty-four hours in the little span we've been given to live.

I remember talking with Joe about the way in which his troubles were overwhelming him. He was feeling the economic squeeze and was trying to run two businesses. Either job would have been sufficiently challenging for someone with average energy, but Joe was not average. Highly motivated, very ambitious, he felt that he could get there twice as fast if he could juggle two careers.

25

In addition to Joe's demanding jobs, he had a family that needed him. His teenage son and daughter were in high school and going through some crucial experiences of their own. They needed a dad who was present for them.

Joe's wife felt so neglected by her husband, so alone with the children that she had grown sullen and resentful. She no longer found it easy to be affectionate and supportive of her husband.

One day Joe bottomed out. He told me his mind was like a TV picture that wouldn't stop rolling. "If I can't make it focus on one picture," he said, "I believe I'll go insane."

You and I have discovered by this time that when our adversaries come at us one at a time, somehow we can defeat them. It's only when we mentally let them overwhelm us by their numbers that we begin to get a feeling of being out of control and somehow in over our heads.

In contrast to Joe, another person dealt with her burdens differently. She had joined our church several months prior to her telephone call. On this day, she called my office saying, "Bill, could you come out to see us?" I could tell by her voice that she really needed to see me, so I proceeded to make a pastoral call on my new parishioner. She told me an unforgettable story. She said she wanted to talk to me because just about this time of year some years ago her husband and their two little boys went fishing. They went to their grandfather's fishpond and took a little rowboat out fishing. She had stayed behind because she was more than eight months pregnant at the time. Somehow, when they finished fishing and were about to get back onto the dock, one of the boys pushed the boat as he stepped out and fell into the water, and her husband and the other son went in after him, and nobody knows how, but all three of them drowned. She lost them all only ten feet from safety. She said, "When I heard their screams and discovered what had happened, the shock of it sent me into labor and the little girl for which we had prayed was born the same day I lost the rest of my family. Every time I celebrate her birthday, I am almost overwhelmed by the grief that floods over my soul because it is also the anniversary of the death of my husband and our two little boys." She continued, "I need you to pray with me." And as her grief washed over me, I asked, "How do you stand the pain? How do you deal with it year after year after year?" She said, "Pastor, I deal with it one day at a time with God's help, and on that particular day, I face it one minute at a time, almost one second at a time." I realized as I knelt and prayed with her that she had discovered a great secret. She put her hand in God's hand and faced all her tomorrows with her hand in his, with a solemn declaration that together they would face it one day at a time.

The beautiful part about facing life as Jesus calls us to face it is that he's there to meet us and help us do it. Indeed, the Bible has promised us strength to deal with all of that which we face today. The Bible says, "As your days, so shall your strength be" (Deut. 33:25, RSV). Isaiah said, "Thou wilt keep him in perfect peace, whose mind is stayed on thee: because he trusteth in thee" (26:3, KJV). How is it that we have such a glorious promise that, no matter what overtakes us in this life, Christ can help us face it?

Several years ago I had an opportunity to go to the Masters Golf Tournament in Augusta, Georgia, gratefully receiving one of those precious tickets. I

27

took my place with the multitude standing about the number-one tee watching the pros as they drove their balls down that first fairway. The first hole at the Masters is probably the most difficult of all, especially with a huge crowd watching. As each golfer approaches the tee box, the announcer begins to speak of the golfer's credentials, his victories, etc., over the blaring PA system. Even the coolest professional can be rattled by such an experience!

I watched one of the famous golfers as he approached his first drive. In watching him, I learned why he is such an outstanding golfer. Just as he was teeing up the ball and beginning his backswing, an ambulance came into the driveway of the clubhouse with all of its sirens screaming. All of the spectators were almost swept off their feet as our ears were bombarded by the sound of that ambulance. I was amazed to see that the pro was so locked in on the ball, so focused on what he was doing, that apparently he didn't even hear that ambulance! If he heard it, it certainly was not obvious in the way he swung at that ball. He drove it three hundred yards down the middle of that fairway! I saw in his concentration the difference between a great golfer and a mediocre golfer.

All great people who live effective lives have the ability to concentrate. They have the same distractions the rest of us have, but somehow they stay locked in on the "one thing needful" and the distractions lose their power over them.

Sometimes we make the same mistake the ten spies made when they gave their report on the land of Canaan to Moses. As the ten men spoke of what they had seen in the land Moses intended for them to conquer, they let their fears get the upper hand, and they began to describe the inhabitants of the land as giants. Alongside the giants, the spies believed themselves to be like grasshoppers. Their experience is a classic example of people who see God, but who see all of their problems first.

When I was a child, I never missed an opportunity to go with my father to Macon, Georgia. A part of the excitement of that hundred-mile trip was the ride up "magic" hill. Somewhere between Cochran and Macon there was a hill that was any little boy's delight. If your father had the time and was inclined to humor you, you could persuade him to stop the car, take it out of gear, release the brake and the car would roll back up the hill. It was miraculous! My brother and I would squeal with delight each time the car rolled up the hill. Following our little adventure, my father would continue the journey to Macon, and later in the same day, we would head toward home. This time we would be traveling south. As we approached "magic" hill, we learned that what we had been seeing from the other direction was an optical illusion. We thought we had been rolling up a hill, an incredible feat. Instead, it only appeared to be a hill. In reality, we had been rolling down the hill, the most natural occurrence in the world!

When our problems overwhelm us and we feel confused and bewildered by them, it may be that we are seeing our problems first and our Savior second. From one perspective, one direction, everything seems impossible. However, if by faith we can turn it around and see God first, and all our problems through him, then we can be like Caleb and Joshua who reassured the frightened spies, "Our enemies have no defense; the Lord is with us. We are well able to overcome!"

All preachers have favorite hymns. Ask them what it is today, though, and it may be different from their choice a year ago. At this present time, my favorite hymn is "Ask Ye What Great Thing I Know." That hymn has a special meaning for me because we sang it on the first Sunday I was in my new pulpit, the First United Methodist Church in Houston. I said my prayers before that first Sunday in Houston . . . many prayers! I spent long hours in careful preparation for the first sermon I wanted to preach from that great pulpit. I had not taken lightly the knowledge that I would be preaching to the largest Methodist congregation in the world and would also be following the best known Methodist preacher in the world, Dr. Charles L. Allen. All of those realizations had made me anything but flippant and casual about my preparation. Still, when that morning hour came and I sat in the pulpit waiting for Dr. Allen to introduce me to the people to whom he had preached for twenty-three wonderful years, I felt totally inadequate. I didn't think myself ready to preach. I thought it was dreadful that all of my preparation and all of my prayers had not been enough. Then the congregation stood and started to sing that glorious hymn, "Ask Ye What Great Thing I Know." During the singing of that hymn, I realized that I had made one of the oldest mistakes anyone can make. I had been thinking about my fears and my apprehensions, focusing on them instead of on the Christ. With his help I was able to see him first, and when I did, the fears and anxiety didn't disappear, but I was given a measure of power over them. When the congregation sat down after the singing of the hymn, I almost ran to the pulpit because I had focused on him. I had centered on the one person who has promised us power in the hour of need and trial.

Christ can make us ready for each day's need. Trust him then, just for today. Today's troubles are enough for one day. Iron with the iron that's hottest!

# III

# Our Mislaid Lord

## *Looking for Christ*

You don't have to wait another moment to begin looking for Christ. It is possible for you to begin right now. Remember God's love for us means that he is already reaching out for you. I want to tell you of two incidents that may help you.

They were our neighbors and our friends. We had lived in the same city with them for several years. He was a leader in our church; he was a senior pilot with a large airline company, and was an asset to the community. He and Susan had two daughters. One of them had graduated from college and had started her own family. The other daughter was a senior in college. Now that this couple had reached their early fifties, they were seeing an end to the economic drain of having children in college and making house payments, and the like, and were about to turn the corner. Within only a few years now they could begin to feather the nest that would keep them warm and secure down into the future years. And then suddenly there was that unexpected visit from someone in the parent company, and the crushing news that there would be a merger of companies and he would be prematurely retired. That good job was gone.

I remember the pathos in Susan's voice when she

called me and asked if I could come. When I got there I saw a strong man who now had a wild look in his eyes to which I could not effectively speak. I remember praying with him, and then having his wife lead me into the next room to show me all of the firearms in the house. She asked me to take those guns home with me because she had seen her depressed husband staring at them. This man was in deep grief because his job, by which he had really defined much of his life, and in which he had found security and standing and stability and so many other things, was suddenly no more. As stress points are counted, the loss of one's position stands high on the list, almost touching the stress that comes when someone loses a spouse or a loved one. Perhaps you have been there.

The second incident is still more tragic. Though we had moved to a distant city, I kept a special relationship with a young physician whom I admired greatly. Bob had come to be a member of the church I served while he was still an intern. Even during those days and nights when the physical drain was tremendous, he worked with our young people on Sunday night. He taught Sunday school on Sunday morning. He carried his beeper and sometimes he had to hustle off to the hospital, but he was there. I marveled at him. I said, "How do you do that?" He replied, "Bill, don't accept those old excuses about people not having time. People can do what they want to do. People can do what they're committed to doing." He added, "I can be here. I may get interrupted, but I can at least try to be in my church." Why, he even tithed on borrowed money! I said, "Bob, are you sure you want to do that? I know you don't have any income." He said, "I have to do it. God has been so good to me. I have a beautiful wife; I have three lovely children. I cannot begin to pay him back for all he's done for me." That's the kind of man he was.

I remember the Saturday when his friends and mine started calling me and telling me about the accident. His wife and two children had been driving along a main thoroughfare, and someone who had had three or four too many drinks veered over the center line and crashed into them head-on. It was a dreadful, horrible accident. The children were cut, bruised, multilated, and broken. They were in intensive care, and no one knew if they would survive. As it turned out, they did live, but barely. The hospital staff thought the mother only had minor injuries. They didn't realize she was hemorrhaging internally, and when they discovered it, it was too late and she was suddenly gone.

All this horrible sequence of events I heard by long distance. I kept waiting. I sat beside the phone, because I knew when there was time, when he could leave the children, his call would come. And it did.

He said, "Bill, I had to hear from you." I thought, as I tried to address that situation, "You don't really want to hear from me, not my halting, stumbling words." I couldn't find the right words, and nobody else could. What he really wanted to hear was a word from God: "When I'm facing the loss of my wife, when I'm facing the hurt to my children, where is my Christ in the middle of all this?"

That's also what the man wanted to know who had lost his job. He couldn't frame the question so precisely, but that's what he wanted to know: "Where is Christ in the middle of my loss? Where is he?"

Mary framed that question in the garden almost two thousand years ago, and you may be one of the millions who have echoed the same refrain: "Tell me where he is. I had a Lord, but my Lord has been mislaid. He has disappeared. In the middle of my grief, in my hurt, in my disappointment, I cannot find him. Please tell me where to find my Lord."

Are you looking in the right place? I know that this can feel very discouraging to you. God seems so far away when we need him sometimes. People even framed the question first in the New Testament, "Why are you searching for the living among the dead?" Mary came to the tomb in order to anoint the cold, lifeless body of a crucified Lord. She came looking for the living among the dead. That's the wrong place to look. We affirm the authenticity of Jesus; we affirm the historical Christ. There is the same kind of hard evidence that Jesus lived as evidence that George Washington existed. We have the same kinds of evidence. I do not know any thoughtful person who will deny that Jesus of Nazareth lived. There is more than adequate documentation to prove that he lived. You just have to come to terms with that.

So, we affirm the historical Christ. But if we look for Jesus only in the past, if all we can do is prepare him for his burial, to bring some spices and ointments, pay our respects to a dead Lord, then there isn't any excitement in that, and we'll never find him. What we must do is come to meet Jesus with a warm and living devotion, because he is alive. He is a present reality; he meets us in our hurt and calls our names, just as he called Mary's. She could not find him because she was looking for him in the wrong places. We do not find him in history. We do not find him in that which grows yellow with age and crumbles at the touch, nor in artifacts or geological finds.

This is a basic spiritual truth that is rediscovered

frequently. If we open our hearts to him, we will find him in his living reality. We will then experience a living Lord—a Lord who makes his history come alive. He makes the Scripture pages exciting, and makes our lives an adventure because he infuses them with his living spirit and power.

Let your imagination go back to Jesus again. He is someone who has felt the pinch of poverty, someone who knows what it's like not to have a salary or a home, someone who knows what it's like to trust God for the next meal, someone who knows what it's like to walk the dusty paths of every conceivable journey, every conceivable circumstance; he has been in and through them all. And he, that understanding Lord, stands with all of his power ready to help you in your grief. He is at your elbow calling your name.

Do you remember that dreadful scene in the book of Kings when the Syrians had besieged the city, and cut off all of its supplies? The inhabitants were beginning to resemble animals rather than persons. They had been without food for so long that they would even sell the head of a donkey for a fortune. In addition to that, they were actually practicing cannibalism. The king overheard two women arguing over which child was to be killed and eaten. When the king heard them, he was so overcome with grief that he rent his garment. And the people were overcome with amazement as they saw that their king did not live in silk and pleasure as they had thought, but actually wore scratchy sack cloth over an emaciated body. Their king was with them in their suffering. That was the last thing they expected.

Jacob, fleeing from his brother's wrath, sleeps with a stone pillow. Isn't that graphic? Don't you know what it's like when you're in a condition of brokenness, when you're in a state of grief over all that you've lost, don't you know what it's like to sleep with a stone for a pillow? Those are horrible nights. But during that dreadful ordeal, the Lord gave Jacob a vision. He saw a ladder extending from heaven to earth and realized that the angels of God were both ascending and descending. He heard those comforting words, "Jacob, I am the God of your father, and I am your God, too. And my hand, my strong right hand, will guide you through this ordeal and I'm going to do for you all that I have promised. No matter how dark the night may be right now, I'm going to carry you through the night. I'll bring you out on the other side." Jacob was so overwhelmed, he was so moved, that he promised the Lord he was going to tithe, and he named the place Bethel, which means the house of God. Jacob said, "The Lord was in this place and I didn't even know it."

My point is this: even if you have been looking for Christ in the wrong places, he is closer to you than you realize. He is there. He is calling your name even though you don't see him. You may not have heard him yet because you were looking for someone who was far away. He's never far away; however, he's speaking to you right now, heart to heart, spirit to spirit. Mary said, "Tell me where you have laid him, and I will take him away" (John 20:15, RSV). Somehow she was saying, "If in my hurt and in my disappointment I could just see him, it would be all right."

Did you read about Florence Chadwick? She tried to swim the English Channel, and she almost made it. In fact, she asked to be taken out of the water just a few hundred yards from the shore. The people who had watched her courageous attempt said, "Why couldn't you make it? You had swum for miles. Why didn't you make those last few yards?" She said, "I would have made it, but a fog bank moved in and I couldn't see the shore. If I could have seen the shore, I could have made it." Mary was saying, "If I can just see him, I can make it."

I like the story that came out of the First World War when a soldier said to his captain, "Where is God?" There they were in the middle of the tangled barbed wire and the muddy foxholes. Men were fighting and snarling like animals in that trench warfare, and that soldier looked into the face of his captain and said, "Would you tell me, sir, where is God in all of this?" And that captain, looking across no man's land through that mud and barbed wire, saw a courageous medic rushing with a companion to aid a wounded soldier who was groaning in his pain. That captain said to the soldier, "There goes God, there he is, don't you see him?"

God shows himself to us in so many ways if we only have eyes to see him. He is there. But, you say, "Don't just tell me God shows himself through other people." I'm not saying that. God has his own unique ministry of presence in addition to his revelation through other people. God, through his holy spirit, stands at our elbow and calls our name.

I never shall forget the man who told me how he came to the chancel one Sunday to receive communion. There was no room in his heart for love right then because the grief he felt over the loss of his son had devastated him. It was more than he could bear. He said, "Before I received the sacrament, however, as I knelt and prayed, I had the distinct feeling that a larger presence stood right behind me. As I prayed in my grief, he put his hand on my shoulder. I can almost feel the warmth still. He put his hand on my shoulder and said, 'Don't worry about your boy. He's with me.' "

"And," the man said, "I live my life in the strength of that knowledge."

Wonderful knowledge, indeed. Oh, if I could only see him, I could make it through my troubles. Even as she wept, he was calling her name, "Mary, here I am, Mary. Don't you remember me?"

How is it we experience spiritual amnesia? We can feel so close to God and then unexpectedly, circumstances jerk the rug out from under us, and we suddenly forget everything. We even forget how to pray. All of those glorious promises are no more. How could she forget that Jesus had said, "I won't leave you alone. If I go away I will come back. I won't leave you like orphans. I won't desert you. I tell you the truth. I will come back and I will abide with you forever." How could she forget that? She had forgotten who he was. She had forgotten whose she was.

When I think about amnesia, I think about Mr. Sutherland. Did you read Mr. Sutherland's story? Someone gave me an old *Time* magazine dating back to the fifties. In that magazine there was an article entitled "The Vigil." It was about a man who was all alone, save for his son, Wilfred Sutherland. This man received the news one day that his only son had been shot down over Holland during the war. It was not known whether he bailed out and survived or whether he went down in the wreckage and died. Mr. Sutherland carried the hope in his heart that perhaps somehow, miraculously, Wilfred had survived.

On Easter morning, 1948, Mr. Sutherland was hurrying across and through the crowd at Kings Cross Station in London on his way to church services, when suddenly he saw across that great multitude a familiar face. He believed it to be the face of his son. For a moment there, their eyes locked, and Mr. Sutherland thought there was a glimmer of recognition. But then the man he believed to be his son turned on his heel, walked into the crowd and was lost to him. Mr. Sutherland believed his son was alive. He believed he had seen him and felt that his son was suffering some kind of amnesia. He withdrew all of his savings and began to spend his weeks and months enlarging pictures of his son and carrying them all over England and Scotland, plastering them in every place where people congregate. Below the picture of his son, he put his own name, address, and telephone number, believing, hoping, praying that his son would see that poster, remember whose son he was and come back to his father. Then, every Easter morning he stood in Kings Cross Station. He had been doing that for ten years when they wrote his story. I do not know whether he was alive this past Easter or not. He would be a very old man if alive, but if he is still living I know where he was, because fathers don't quit on their sons when their sons are lost. Don't give up yet. Christ is already closer than you realize. He will find you as you are finding him. You should think of it this way: there is another Father, who, through Jesus Christ, has put up posters all over for you. He is whispering your name, waiting for you to acknowledge him and turn and say, "Master, Master." Have you acknowledged his presence in the middle of your loss, in the middle of your hurt? Shouldn't you do that today?

# IV

## Our God—The Last of the Big Spenders

### *Your Heart Can Experience God's Presence*

If God is so close, why can't I feel him near me? Part of the problem is our own culture. Sometime ago an unusual advertisement was run in a Hollywood newspaper. It seems that the ad was seeking an attractive young woman who would be willing to appear on stage in Hollywood. The nature of the ad was not unusual in that sense, because there are many standing in line to be Hollywood stars. But this article went on to say they were searching for a young woman who would be willing to have her wrists slashed in front of a camera. Medics would be standing by, the best in medical assistance available, for they were searching for someone who would move beyond the category of acting into the realm of reality in terms of intense, bloody suffering.

The ad represents a problem which is becoming more and more serious in any form of entertainment. People are not so easily shocked any more. We've seen the movies run the gamut. You may have gone to see the movie *Jaws* a few years ago. Remember the great shark? I saw an ad about *Jaws* once on a marquee of a theater. Someone had made a great big papier-mache shark that must have been twenty feet long. In the open mouth there was a large doll with its legs protruding.

After the exploitation of great fish or animals, the movies turned to natural disasters like *Earthquake* or to fires like *The Towering Inferno*. Now we see kinky and bizarre problems like incest and homosexuality. The human body has been exploited about as much as it can be in the movies. The last taboos are now being exploited for the sake of entertainment. All of this points to the difficulty of getting through to people whose hearts have been toughened. It takes more and more to make us react, to create a ripple on our emotions. We aren't so easily shocked anymore.

One of the problems with our culture is that the sensational isn't sensational. The spectacular isn't spectacular anymore. Those things that once moved us no longer faze us. We see fifty thousand people killed on the highways. Half of them are killed by drivers who thoughtlessly drive while drinking and the laws we have on the books to prevent that kind of thing from happening are so weak and insensitive to human suffering that they almost mock compassion.

This is the point where something else may be involved with your feelings about the sensational events. It could be your own sense of personal pain. I once had an opportunity to speak to Compassionate Friends. You may know about this unusual organization. In order to be a part of it you have to have suffered the loss of a child. You have to declare your name and your hurt at the beginning of the meeting. As I sat and listened to their painful expressions of grief, my first impulse was to ask myself, "What on earth am I doing here?" I couldn't begin to plumb the depths of the suffering I heard being expressed all over that room, and I felt like an outsider. I heard a

41

mother talk about her son who was killed by someone who was driving while intoxicated. As I listened to her story, I thought, that mother can be multiplied by thousands all over the country.

There may be a tragedy like this in your own life that has left you feeling numb. It may be one reason that the sensational isn't sensational anymore for you. There may be so much hurt that you don't feel as you once did. There are thousands still trying to come to terms with the loss of a child, with the grandchildren they'll never have, with the Christmases that are somehow never complete. If you are one of these you may be struggling with questions like, "How can I go on living? How can I keep my nose above the water?" Something subtle (but sad) has happened to our souls in that we don't feel as we once felt. Some blame our callous natures on the media. They say that with violence of every kind being piped into our living rooms, it's no wonder that we lose our sensitivity. But it is far more than that. Intensely personal suffering can make us numb from the hurt that we have experienced.

Even our children are less sensitive today. I suspect that this comes from too much media sensation plus some personal hurt. I can remember an event in my childhood when I saw a wreck in front of my grandmother's house in which a man's arm was practically torn off. This was before the time of air-conditioned automobiles, and he was riding with his arm out of the window when he sideswiped another car. After I saw that accident, there were many nights when I was awakened by bad dreams, and my mother would come in and comfort me. I haven't had a nightmare like that in a long time. I doubt my children would have nightmares like that with all that they've seen and with all that they've been exposed to.

I can remember when the most exciting thing that happened in our home in the evening was my father telling us a scary story, and by scary, I'm talking about wolves, and bears, and tigers, and things like that. We always had a hero at our house, a little yearling whose name was Little White Face. Always, when we were cornered by a bear or a lion in my father's stories, Little White Face would come galloping out of nowhere, chase the creature off and let us ride on his back triumphantly back to the house. I thought Little White Face was the greatest thing in the world. I decided that when I had children I was going to tell them about Little White Face. When my wife and I had children, I started pouring these stories into them that I'd heard from my father. When I had to be out of town, I'd put them on tape so Jean could play them to the children before they went to bed. But after a time, the children became bored with my stories. They discovered TV on Saturday morning, and when my wife and I were trying to sleep, the children were in there turning on the television set. I remember my son dragging me out of bed early one morning. He took me into the den, saying, "Daddy, I can't fix the television set. Will you fix it?"

And I fiddled with it for a time, and all I could get was a test pattern, and I looked at the clock and I said, "My soul, son, the television station isn't up yet! It isn't even on. All there is for a picture is this test pattern."

He said, "Yes, Daddy, but if you fix it just right you can hear that ummmm!" What chance did I have with my old stories in the face of Saturday morning?

A second part of our problem is the numbness that comes from our own inner pain. Sybil was a beautiful girl who lived alone. She attended church, but the church's message had not registered with her. She was popular with the young men, but for the wrong reason. Feeling very unloved, Sybil was easily exploited by any man who said he loved her.

Sybil's parents had divorced when she was eight years old. They didn't fight over custody; in fact, they left their little girl with the distinct impression that neither of them enjoyed being with her. They never shared the moments of success and recognition that Sybil garnered during her growing up years. Their agenda was too crowded to include a class play or a chapel program.

Somehow, Sybil finished college, but her heart was not in her work. The huge void within her was the result of a lack of any real love. Moreover, there was a quality of meanness in Sybil, a self-defense mechanism, to insulate her from additional hurt. Sybil's heart had, without her realizing it, grown spiritually numb. Her sensitivity to God had become calloused, and her heart was caught up within its own hurt. However, this sensitivity to God's presence can be restored. You learn that he is near in spite of all that you have experienced. God can remove that numbness from your heart.

Sometime ago, some sheep ranchers out West came up with the solution to an age-old problem—a problem that concerned the mother sheep and her lamb. When the ranchers let the ewe and her lamb go out to graze in early winter, the mother sheep wouldn't feel the drop in temperature or the snow falling. She would continue to walk and forage until, finally, the little lamb would die of exposure. The ranchers struggled with this problem. How on earth could they get the ewe to come back to the safety of the barn? Finally, they came upon a very practical solution. They brought all of those sheep into the corral, and taking some electric clippers, they quickly shaved the wool from between the ears of the sheep, exposing the tops of their heads, and then released them. This time, as the sheep walked across the plains, with the temperatures plummeting and the snow falling, for the first time in their lives, they felt it, and when they felt it, they went back to the barn and took the little ones with them.

The time has come for you to allow God to get at the wool of your heart. You have probably insulated yourself against the public violence and the personal pain. You need God to enable you to feel again. You can apply personally the promise of Ezekiel, who spoke for God when he said, "A new heart I will give you . . . I will take out of your flesh the heart of stone and give you a heart of flesh" (Ezek. 36:26, RSV). And when the numbness has been taken from your souls, then you will truly hear that verse, "For God so loved the world, that he gave his only begotten Son" (John 3:16, KJV). When you hear that verse, perhaps in a deeper way than you have ever heard it, everything inside your soul will begin to sing.

I wonder how the disciples reacted when they first heard it. I wish we could have captured it on video tape. I wish there could have been some kind of meter put on them to see how they reacted inwardly when Jesus said, "Look, I didn't come into the world to condemn the world. I came that the world might be saved. I want all who believe in the Son to have eternal life. That's why I came. I came to love. I came to save. God's other name is love." I wonder if the meter

would have gone all the way over and locked on the
other side. Or, I wonder if perhaps it would give just a
little twitch as if the disciples had heard but didn't
really hear.

Do you suppose that the enormity of what God has
done for us in Christ could ever be completely lost on
us? Do you think we could ever reach the point where
somehow it doesn't register that the Almighty God
has sent his only Son to die for us? I don't think so. I
think God wants to make us like Saint Paul, who never
could forget the enormity of God's love. Paul said,
with incredulous awe, "While we were yet sinners
Christ died for us." Christ didn't wait for us to be
worthy, to understand it all, or to make ourselves
sufficiently sensitive. He came while we were *all* too
numb inside. He died for us that we might be saved.

During the summer of 1983, after a very slow start,
the Houston Astros began winning their games
regularly. During their winning streak, a merchant on
one of the city's main thoroughfares erected a sign
which read: "Astros welcome here as long as they
keep winning."

Now that's the final touch, the ultimate rejection,
isn't it? As long as you keep winning you're welcome
here. But, the great good news is what Jesus said to
those disciples and still says to us: "It doesn't matter
whether you're a winner or whether you're a loser. It
doesn't matter whether you know me very well or not.
I died for you! I gave my life for you. I am for you and
being for you is not contingent on how saintly you are.
I am for you!"

Roy Smith grew up out on the plains of Kansas
when times were very hard. His father worked in the
mill—never made more than a few dollars a week. Roy
Smith said it was hard for his parents to scrape up

enough money for him to go to college, but he wanted to go to that little college in his hometown—a Methodist college—and somehow or other his parents managed to get him enrolled. Then Roy was given a part in a debate that would put him on stage. More than anything else in the world, he wanted a new pair of shoes for the big day. Somehow, out of their meager income, his parents managed to buy some new shoes for their son. Just before Roy went on stage, someone burst through the doors of the auditorium and shocked him with the news that his father had been hurt badly in an accident at the mill. Roy Smith ran down the streets of that little town into the mill, but it was too late. His father had died. They buried him the next day, a cold and windy day, and then Roy Smith went back to the mill to get his father's tools and the coveralls that he'd been wearing at the time of the accident. Someone had thoughtfully put all of them into the tool box his father had used. They had carefully folded the bloody coveralls, and then had placed his old brogans bottom side up there in the box. When Roy Smith opened the lid of that box, the first thing he saw was his father's shoes. Those shoes had holes in the bottom that stretched from side to side. In that second, he realized that while he stood in his new shoes, his father had stood on the cold steel of that mill floor in shoes that didn't protect his feet. Roy Smith said he felt a numbness around his heart (*Tales I Have Told Twice,* Nashville: Abingdon Press, 1964).

Frankly, that is not the kind of numbness or callousness that we have been discussing. The "numb" feelings Roy Smith sensed were the birth pangs of new life. You can sense them in the future too. You can begin to feel again with a new realization of what God has done for us in Christ.

Several times when my mother came to visit, we made a little pilgrimage to the cemetery where our loved ones are buried. Each time we went there, we looked at Grandmother's and Grandfather's resting places, and then the grave of my father and the vacant place for my mother. Just to the right of where she will be is a little stone marking Janelle's grave. There were six in my family, and my sister Janelle died at the age of four. She was the oldest. She died at four with diphtheria—not much they could do in those days. And every time we go to that little cemetery and start to drive away, Mother begins to tell the story of how it was with Janelle. I could say the story backward. I've heard it over and over again. She doesn't tell it again just because she's growing old. She tells it because she's still doing her grief work, and she sees in her son someone who will do her grief work with her. I realized a long time ago that if my mother had had fifty children instead of six, she would still grieve about Janelle. She will never be complete until she has that entire circle together. She will never be totally herself until she has them all together under her touch, under her wings, as it were.

You say, "Of course that's true with mothers!" Well, if that's true with human love, *how much more the divine love?* If we cannot limit a mother's love, if we understand that it doesn't matter how many children she has, that she loves each one of them as though he/she is the only one she has to love, if we understand that about mothers, why can't we understand about the Heavenly Father? Jesus said, "If you then, who are evil, know how to give good gifts to your children, how much more will your Father who is in heaven give good things to those who ask him!"

(Matt. 7:11, RSV). Think how much more our Heavenly Father can help you to become open to his love.

I remember a family vacation in North Carolina, when we went to see a frontier farm. Part of a huge crowd, we went in to see the cottage. All of our children were small; our youngest was three years old. After we went to see the cottage, we went out to the field to see the barn. Suddenly, Jean and I met out at the barn and experienced that sickening feeling that many parents have known. One look at each other, and in a second, we realized one of the children was missing. (It's the same kind of thing that happened to the parents of Jesus. They each thought the other had him.) In that instant we realized that in that crowd somewhere was a three-year-old. We didn't say anything. I just started running. I started shouting her name. People looked at me like I was crazy. I didn't care. They saw me coming, and they got out of my way like leaves before a storm. They knew I'd run over them! I was going back to that cottage as fast as my feet would carry me. I never ran that fast before. I went through that house, and then I thought about the parking lot. Maybe she had gone to that big parking lot. I ran to the parking lot, and there in the far corner I saw our old station wagon and Cathy. There she stood, with her head about the height of the bumper, with twin rivers of tears flowing down her cheeks. She saw me at the same time I saw her. We met in the middle of that parking lot, and I swept her up in my arms. I couldn't say anything. My flesh literally shook for an hour. I began to understand what Jesus meant when he said, "When one of those who has been lost comes back to the Father, the corridors of heaven ring for joy." The corridors of heaven ring! This is the intense, unfailing love that your Heavenly Father has for you. You can be absolutely sure that he wants you to know his love.

Several years ago I was watching the World Series on TV with Sparky Anderson as the commentator. He was managing the Cincinnati Reds at that time. Sparky was telling about the seventh game of the World Series. He stopped in the middle of his description of the game and said, "Boys and girls, I want you to know the most exciting moment in all of time is the seventh game of the World Series." I wanted to jump up and debate him! I wanted to say, "No, Sparky. No! The most exciting moment of all is when someone who has been insensitive to God, who has not felt his presence for a long time, has that sensation of new life around his heart. The most exciting time for you will be when you feel those birth pangs and know that Christ is very real to you."

Did you read that interview with the astronaut's wife shortly after her husband stepped onto the moon and returned? I'll never forget what she said. The reporter asked the astronaut's wife about the most exciting moment for her.

"Was it when your husband got into orbit?"

She said no.

"How about when he stepped on the moon?"

"No."

He said, "Was it when he redocked?"

"No."

"Was it when they blasted off coming back?"

"No."

He was perplexed. He said, "When, then, was the most exciting moment for you?"

She said, "The most exciting moment was when my loved one put his foot on the deck of that ship!"

That's the greatest moment in all of time for God, when one of his children says, "I've been gone too long. I've tried my way, and it's not working. I'm going to try God's way. I'm going home."

You *can* begin to feel God's presence. You may have been trying to make life go on your own by yourself. Isn't it time for you to turn to him? You can begin by saying simply: Lord, I want to be close to you. I'm coming home.

# V

## God's Mysterious Gift

*How Can I Find Forgiveness?*

Leslie D. Weatherhead once said that the forgiveness of God is the most therapeutic idea in the whole world. Psychological adjustment is wonderful, and we need more of it. But nothing in all the earth which man can do can ever satisfy the human need for forgiveness. It is at the heart of the human problem. Any treatment of the human dilemma that ignores the need for forgiveness at the hands of God is superficial. It leaves the deeper needs of the human spirit untouched and unhealed.

These deep needs often keep us from a full awareness of God's love for us. The path to recognizing God's presence, accepting him in our hearts, usually passes through the doorway of God's forgiveness.

Millions testify that finding forgiveness is the most memorable experience in their lives. Therefore, when someone comes to me with this deeply personal question, "How can I find forgiveness?" I feel that they are almost always on the right track. Many years of counseling people have convinced me that the very act of reaching out for forgiveness, having within our own hearts a sense of sin—a recognition that we need forgiveness—is the first requirement for finding forgiveness. This is the paradox. Finding a heart for God often begins with finding our own sense of heartfelt sin.

Have you noticed that it is fashionable to talk about sin once more? It's always been a very significant word in the Holy Scriptures, but sin has ebbed and flowed as far as its popularity with the human scene. I can recall in the opening days of my ministry going to a seminar where a psychologist chided all of us about our usage of the word *sin*. As the years passed, many people became somewhat reluctant to ever use the word *sin* when speaking about themselves. Then psychiatry rediscovered sin. You may recall Karl Menninger's thoughtful book a few years ago, entitled *Whatever Became of Sin?* About the time we had almost been persuaded we should not talk about our sins so much, the world of psychiatry comes back on the scene with its new discovery concerning sin and reassures us that sin applies to us all.

It seems that the old word *guilt* is available for us again, too. I'm talking about what is often called *good guilt*. We all know about the bad kind. Lots of people can testify to having been guided, disciplined, and motivated by the burden of inflicted guilt. I have a friend who claims his mother was the East Coast distributor of guilt! Lots of us grew up on the stuff, and we react by claiming that we have no real guilt at all. Then psychiatry recovered the positive aspects of guilt. There was true, authentic, realistic guilt. Then there was also false guilt. Nobody should be consumed with false guilt, but then true guilt is not so bad. In fact it can be helpful. It points the way toward a better tomorrow. It leads us upward and onward. It can show us the high road. It can show us the good road. Finally, we've come back again, to the point where the Scriptures have been all along—sometimes guilt is God's hold on our heart. It can be his way of bringing us back to himself.

What this means is that it's psychologically sound to consider the whole concept of forgiveness and the fact that all of us must have within us a sense of sin. It may well guide us to find forgiveness.

The Scriptures have always guided readers in this way. A very familiar line says, "All have sinned and fall short of the glory of God" (Rom. 3:23, RSV). Indeed, Scripture teaches us that we're engaging in self-deception if we tell ourselves we have no sin. We're lying to ourselves. We've substituted a falsehood for the truth. More than that, not only do we tell ourselves something that isn't true, but we make God a liar. Our claim to complete righteousness is contrary to the most profoundly inspired idea of Scripture. It means that there is none righteous. No, not one.

Isaiah said, "All we like sheep have gone astray; we have turned every one to his own way" (Isa. 53:6, RSV). The Scriptures have said this repeatedly, and it's good that we have come back to the recognition that there is an inherent problem in the human situation that cries out for forgiveness.

Sometimes we've comforted ourselves with what could be called "horizontal comparisons." We like to do that. A horizontal comparison is made when we rely on another person, rather than on God's will as our standard. It happens to us all the time. In many ways we resemble one another, and we can compare ourselves with our friends and say, "Look, I'm just as big and just as strong and just as holy as that person is."

Even Simon Peter tried it when the Lord was confronting him with his failure. The Lord asked him,

"Simon, do you love me?" And he asked Simon not just once, but repeatedly. Simon was squirming beneath that penetrating gaze, and he tried to shift some of the shame of his own failure onto John. He said, "Lord, what about this one? He didn't come off too well himself. Let's talk about his sins for a little while." And Jesus said, "What is that to you, Simon? I'm not talking to John; I'm talking to you." We've always found comfort in horizontal comparisons. The only problem with that is that the Scripture doesn't leave that option open to us.

Augustine felt pretty good about himself when he compared his morality to that of his fellows at the University of Carthage. He thought he was a good, pure, noble, young man. Then Augustine said, "One day Jesus of Nazareth crossed my path, and I saw what a terrible mess I'd made." In the white light of Jesus' character, we see ourselves for who we really are. Those horizontal comparisons comfort us, while a comparison with the Christ convicts us.

Sometimes Jesus begins to move in your heart before you know it. He brings a sense of need into your life. Your work loses its appeal. Small irritations at home grow into major problems. You sense that there must be something better. I wonder if, without realizing it, you have begun to see yourself in and through the eyes of Christ. The impact of Christ before you are even conscious of him often leads you to become aware of your tremendous need.

In the second place, the Lord helps you to look even deeper within your own heart. He helps you to discover what he alone can show you, that finding forgiveness involves the acknowledgment of sin. This is perhaps his most delicate and holy surgery. He gently guides you to acknowledge that you have failed not just yourself but him. "If we confess our sins," the Bible says, "he is faithful and just and will forgive our sins and cleanse us from all unrighteousness" (I John 1:9, RSV).

Well, you say, "That bothers me. Why should God want me to spell it out? The Bible says God knows my mind and my heart. He understands my thoughts from afar. Surely he knows what I am feeling. I feel like an idiot getting on my knees and confessing my sins to God. Why should I confess my sins? He knows my need already!"

Of course he knows your need. He knows my need, too. The catch is, he wants us to know it. He's waiting until we recognize our need. He's waiting until it's plain to us. In our recognition of our need for him, in the moment of confessing that need, we open wide the doors of our hearts and his miraculous work is done.

Mr. Jones needed just that kind of work. He hobbled through the door and slumped in a chair in the pastor's study. Beside him were the two canes that enabled him to walk. Mr. Jones had used those canes for more than twenty-five years, ever since the awful days of World War II when he served his country in France. His wife and family, indeed the entire community, accommodated Mr. Jones' volatile temper and irascible disposition because they could only imagine the suffering that accompanies a war wound of the kind that crippled him. On that day, however, Mr. Jones wanted to deal with another wound—a burdened soul. He had not been wounded in the war, he confessed. He had been crippled by a venereal disease. He had lived a lie all of those years and every person whose life touched his had been affected by his lie. "Can God forgive me?" he inquired. Gradually,

God's miraculous work had led him to open the doors of his heart and to look for God's grace.

Do you remember the people in the Scriptures who gave Jesus the most trouble? It was not the real sinner. It was certainly not even the people who knew that they were sinners. Rather, it was the people who somehow put themselves above the ordinary in terms of their morality. Jesus told them a story one day. He said, "Once a Pharisee and a Publican went to the temple to pray. The Pharisee said, as he prayed thus with himself, 'I thank thee, Lord, that I am not as other men. I fast. I pay my tithes, I keep the law. I do all of those things a separated one is supposed to do. (That's what the word *Pharisee* means, the "separated one.") I do all these things, Lord. I'm so grateful I'm not like this wretched Publican, that sorry sinner yonder on the back row of the temple.' "

Jesus said all the while the Pharisee was praying like that, the poor Publican was saying, "Oh Lord, have mercy on me, a sinner." That man did not even look up, but instead looked down at the floor and kept on saying, "Oh Lord, have mercy on me, a sinner." Jesus said, "The Publican went home a justified man." Not even God can forgive someone who doesn't feel the need for forgiveness. If you are faithful in confessing your sins, he will forgive your sins.

About the son whom she was to bear, Mary said, "He has filled the hungry with good things, and the rich he has sent empty away" (Luke 1:53, RSV). He will fill the poor and the hungry, the paupers in spirit, but he will send the rich away empty. In other words, if you feel that you have everything you need, he cannot do anything for you.

Many people say Jesus never used sarcasm. I had a professor once who said that on occasion Jesus did use sarcasm. He argues that when Jesus said, "The well have no need of a physician," he was being sarcastic. When the Pharisees and the Sadducees were giving Jesus a hard time for being the friend of sinners, prostitutes, and tax collectors, they murmured against him, saying, "Behold . . . a friend of . . . sinners" (Matt. 11:19*b*). Jesus said, "I came to heal the sick; the well have no need of a physician." He may have been sarcastic, because who is well? It's the teaching of the Scriptures that everyone needs the Great Physician. If you do not feel that you need him, if you somehow feel yourself beyond all of that talk about redemption, then you need him most of all.

Alexander Maclaren addressed this point when he told the story about the jar lowered into the ocean. He said, "You can take a jar, lower it tightly capped into the deepest ocean, and when you draw it out again it will be as dry inside as though it had been in an oven" (*The Best of Alexander Maclaren*, New York: Harper & Brothers, 1949). You can live all of your life surrounded by an ocean of God's love. His redemption work is done. Jesus has died on the cross. The work of forgiveness is complete. It's done! You can live all of your life surrounded by an ocean of love, but if you do not open yourself to that love, it will never fill your life. Scripture says that we open ourselves to that love when we confess our sins. It's one small act we can do—to fling wide the doors of our hearts to receive his redeeming love.

In the third place, as you appropriate forgiveness, you become an avenue for forgiveness. You can now go on to become a kind of channel, through which his forgiveness can flow. You do not need just to talk about the experience of forgiveness in terms of an isolated experience just between God and yourself.

That isn't the way it works. Once the forgiveness of God enters your life it flows through you into the lives of all of those persons who have done you wrong, who have said bad things about you, who have been unkind. Forgiveness is like electricity, which needs to be grounded in order to be effective. Forgiveness can't get into you unless it can get out of you. In order to find the fullest experience of forgiveness, you must become a channel through which forgiveness can flow. If you are willing to be a channel of forgiveness, responding to God's miraculous work within, you can enter a new dimension of forgiveness.

It isn't easy to be a forgiving person. It isn't easy at all—to be really forgiving. I was reminded of that the other day by one of my favorite philosophers. Do you know the little cartoon character named Andy Capp, the one whose wife's name is Flo? Andy has a vicar whom he dodges all the time. He dodges his pastor because he is always in the pub and never in the church. One day when Flo, for the umpteenth time, decides to take Andy back home again, the vicar commends Flo saying, "Flo, I'm so glad you took him back again."

And Flo says, "There's something about me; I just have to forgive and forget."

Behind his hand, Andy says, "There's something about her, all right. She never forgets that she forgives!"

It's so hard to turn an offense loose. The other day *Time* had as its lead story, the account of the Pope's forgiveness of his would-be assassin. I enjoyed reading the letters to the editor that followed in later issues. The next issue contained a very revealing letter—it was just a line: "It is the Pope's business to forgive."

You say to me, "All of this about forgiveness, it is God's business to forgive his children." Certainly it is, but on this business of forgiveness he has put a condition. The condition is stated every time we pray the Lord's Prayer: "Forgive us our trespasses as we forgive those who trespass against us." They are always linked together. However, this condition is for your ultimate benefit. It will lead you into the fullest dimension of forgiveness: that which will link forgiveness from your Heavenly Father with forgiveness for those who have hurt you. If you would find forgiveness you must be willing in your heart of hearts to be a channel of forgiveness.

Finally, God's mysterious grace will help you to trust in his faithfulness. He has clearly stated that if you confess your sins, he is faithful and just to forgive. His justness wouldn't let him break his promise to forgive your sins and to cleanse you of all your unrighteousness. He will help you have faith in his ability to keep his word, to fulfill his promises. You can believe that he does exactly what he promises and see his cross as the sign of his faithfulness. The cross is the guarantee that God does, indeed, keep his promises. The cross is not only the awful symbol of what sin can do, what our sin did—crucify the Lord of glory—but the cross is also the sign of redeeming love. In spite of all that we did to him, he loves us still, and he offers us forgiveness and salvation. I say any experience that reminds you of that ought never be forgotten.

John Bunyan in *Pilgrim's Progress* spoke for millions when he said, "Just as Christian came up to the cross, his burden loosed from off his shoulders, and fell from off his back. . . ." "At the cross, at the cross where I first saw the light, and the burden of my heart rolled away. It was there by faith I received my sight, and now I am happy all the day." The cross is the guarantee!

I was recently asked, "Do you like to hunt quail? Did you ever have any dogs?" It always stirs in me a memory mixed with pain and pleasure because I have had many pairs of hunting dogs. And how I loved them! I always trained them myself, raising them from puppies. That's one of the greatest satisfactions—to see a dog perform really well and to know that you both raised and trained him.

I remember how good my dogs had it. I built a house for them out in the backyard. I had a screened-in run—screened, mind you, not just enclosed with regular wire, but screened wire, so that the mosquitoes and gnats and flies wouldn't bother them during the summer months. I had a bedroom built for them, connected to their run by a walkway. For the winter months I found one of those mats that the clerks stand on at the grocery stores to keep their feet warm. I had gotten one of those thermostatically controlled mats, and I put it against the wall of their bedroom so they could curl up with their backs against it on a cold winter's night. I had an automatic waterer and feeder for them, which fed and watered them perpetually. They even had their own sewage system back over in one corner of the run. One of my members, who thought I was carried away, offered to give me a window unit to cool them in the summer time. My wife, however, put her foot down about that and said she wouldn't pay the electricity bill if I did that! So the dogs had to settle for a revolving fan that cooled their pen during the hot summer days. My dogs had to rough it!

One winter day a friend and I were out hunting with those dogs in some woods where a bulldozer had been at work. The terrain was rough and uneven. We thought the dogs had gone in one direction, and we turned in another direction. We were walking along through waist-high bushes when suddenly a quail flew up and I shot too soon. I shot him before he cleared the bushes. I killed the bird, but with the sound of that shot I heard the yelp of my dogs. I did not know it, did not see them, but they had gone around behind those bushes and had pointed side-by-side right before me. In one of those freakish accidents the shot from my gun went through both of my dogs. They did not die immediately. They managed to get up from the ground. One of them went after the dead bird. That's what he had been trained to do. Just before he picked the bird up and started back to me, he fell to the ground. He died in the act of retrieving. The other one, horribly mutilated, came to me trying to lick my hand in the middle of her pain. I stood there in the agony of what I had done and knew I had to get her out of her misery. I shot her again. I wrapped their bodies in my hunting coat and buried both of them there.

Through that awful experience, the cross became more real to me. If my dogs had snarled and snapped at me, or even if they had run away, if they had been angry, then I could have taken what I had done a lot easier. But the fact remained that they reached out to me and still loved me. The hurt of that experience is the pain we feel in the Cross. Something of the same thing happened on the cross! Jesus Christ suffered the worst we could give him. He went to a cross because of our sins. Our carelessness and our indifference and our unconcern put him there. Yet, in spite of our sin, he said, "Father, forgive them; for they know not what they do" (Luke 23:34, RSV).

He still reaches out in love to you and waits for you to make a response to that love, waits for you to open your heart to that love that he might give you the full gift of forgiveness. This full gift of forgiveness can give you the freedom to open your heart. It can be a new beginning for you.

# VI

## Sometimes He Knocks with Bloody Knuckles

### *Opening Up to God*

When I met Jim, he was sleeping on a pile of rags between two outside air conditioning units. He was only in his early twenties, but the mileage he had put into those years was enough for a much older man.

Jim had started taking drugs during his junior high years. His subsequent unruly conduct forced his parents to shuttle him from one school to the next. When they finally realized the source of his difficulty, they tried rehabilitation therapy, but without success. Their son was incorrigible. In desperation, they cut off his allowance—hoping to end his purchasing drugs. Jim started stealing the family's valuables and pawning them, forcing his parents to padlock everything of value. Jim eventually held up a convenience store; a prison term followed.

Before Jim's sentence was completed, he escaped from prison, but was soon recaptured. Later, when he was finally released, he promptly fell back into his old ways.

Jim's parents were broken by grief. They had been deceived so many times by their son, they were worn out. Every relative and friend had been "conned" and used until they no longer had any hope or trust left.

They felt frustrated and helpless as though all doors had been closed.

Do you remember the old custom regarding doors in rural parts of the country? Before air conditioning the doors were always open in our homes. The screen door was there to be sure, but it was unlatched. And when a neighbor knocked or called to us, the standard response was, "Door's open; come on in." An open door! It isn't surprising then that one of the last images given to us in the Bible is the beautiful picture of Jesus standing, knocking outside a closed door, wanting desperately for someone to open and let him in. "Behold, I stand at the door and knock; if any one hears my voice and opens the door, I will come in to him and eat with him, and he with me" (Rev. 3:20, RSV). Even when we realize that Christ is closer to us than we may have thought, there is still something more. He will help us open our hearts in a way that brings us joy.

Jesus knocks, but he knocks gently. Sometimes we wish he wouldn't be so courteous. In fact we wish our Lord were more like the farmer who, in a desperate attempt to get the mule to do what he wanted to do, slapped him on the head with a two by four, declaring to the people who saw him do it that he just wanted to get the mule's attention. Sometimes we wish God would do that for us—just get our attention. Like the title of that old country song I heard on the radio the other day, "Drop-kick Me, Jesus, through the Goalposts of Life!" Just drop-kick me; don't give me any chance to go to the right or to the left, make me go straight and true. We yearn for him just to take charge and make everything easy and simple. However, paradoxically, even if he did that you would still long for that deeper, personal relationship of the opening heart.

I yearned for some kind of Damascus road experience in which God would just knock me down. Sometimes, without being fully aware of it, we may want a God who will abridge our freedom and break down the door to our lives or even treat us like little children to whom parents say, "Behave yourselves, now, or I'll punish you." We want a deity who will jerk a knot into us and make us shape up. Instead, we have a courteous Christ who knocks every so gently on our heart's door. He will not burglarize our souls, nor short-circuit our freedom. He stands and waits and knocks so softly at our heart's door that we can ignore him if we choose.

Which one of us has not admired Holman Hunt's great picture of "The Light of the World"? I saw it once in all of its glory in Saint Paul's Cathedral. What a place to see it! I stood before that great painting and looked and looked and drank it in. As I looked yet again, I saw that there is no latch on the outside. He knocks with longing in his eyes and across his face, but there is no way he can open the door from without. We are not in any danger of some kind of divine intrusion. Instead, he knows, and we know, that the latch is always on the inside.

When Elijah squatted in the cave on the side of the mountain, God said, "Stand upon the mount before the Lord" (I Kings 19:11, RSV), and Elijah looked and saw wind that smashed the rocks to pieces, but God was not in that wind. He saw an earthquake that rearranged the face of the earth, but God was not in the earthquake. He saw a fire which was devastating in that it consumed all that was before it, but God was not in the fire. After the fire the Bible tells us there was a "still small voice" and God was in the quiet voice. It isn't surprising then that the Bible says if you would know, be still, because this Christ is so courteous he knocks very gently.

See him as he and the two disciples are walking to the little village of Emmaus. They, who had been blinded by their tears and disappointment, are oblivious to who he is, and now they're walking through the little village and they've turned aside into their home. And the Bible tells us Jesus "appeared to be going further" (Luke 24:28, RSV). He was about to go further; he was going on down the road, but they constrained him, inviting him to come in. He would not invite himself in. He waited with exquisite courtesy for the invitation to come from them.

You may be saying, "Yes, perhaps he was once there for me years ago, but how long would he be waiting? I've kept my life closed for so long in so many ways. He probably gave up on me." I want you to know now that though he knocks gently, this Christ of ours knocks with great persistence. He keeps on knocking. Just as he taught his followers to seek and knock and ask, even so, he keeps on seeking and knocking and asking. I tell you, he is relentless in his pursuit of us. Now and again some person who has given way to defeat and despair will say to me in a downcast voice, "God has given up on me." And I have a standard response. I always come back with one strong resounding, "NEVER!" You may have given up on yourself, but God give up on someone? He never does.

When the Bible talks about God's everlasting love, his remembrance of everyone of us, it says, "Can a woman forget her sucking child?" (Isa. 49:15, RSV). We all know the answer to that. Some time ago, Dr. Jim Argue, minister of the Pulaski Heights Methodist Church in Little Rock, Arkansas, finished his sermon a little early and decided he would mention to the people in his viewing audience that Charles Allen was retiring that Sunday. Dr. Allen was bringing to a brilliant conclusion fifty glorious years of service for our Lord's church. Dr. Argue properly noted that monumental contribution and asked his congregation to pray with him a prayer of gratitude. And then he said, "Don't stop there—let's pray for the man who's to follow him. I think he must be a good man to follow Dr. Allen."

Dr. Argue finished the service, spoke to his people, and went home. When he arrived there, the telephone was ringing. A voice on the other end of the line said to him, "Dr. Argue, I want to thank you for what you did this morning, and I want to tell you that I know Bill Hinson is a good man because he's my son." That was my mother who called Dr. Argue. When I got to Houston, I heard the preachers telling that story and I wondered to myself, "Will my mother always remember me like that?" Of course she will. The Bible implies that a mother cannot forget her child, but even if she could, through some kind of sickness, "I will not forget you," God says. "I have graven you on the palms of my hands" (Isa. 49:15b-16, RSV).

Listen to his voice as he pleads through the prophet, saying, "How can I give you up? . . . My heart recoils within me, my compassion grows warm and tender" (Hos. 11:8, RSV). Though we've sinned against him and disregarded his statutes and commandments, he still asks, "How can I give you up?" He is overwhelmed by compassion.

Do you remember how Hosea chose Gomer, a woman of the street, for his wife? He gave her a position in the community. He gave her respect. He gave her his love, his loyalty, his devotion. Do you remember how she became the mother of his children and then returned to her old life? And this time she went so low and stayed so long in her harlotry that he was able to go finally and *buy* her back.

God said, "Hosea, I've done that over and over again. My people never get so low that I don't want them back again. I can never give them up!"

The other day I heard a radio preacher say that 99 percent of today's people are going straight to the devil's hell. And I thought as I listened to him, "This guy has been sitting beside the turnstile counting them." I mean, he sounded so sure about it! Not 97 percent, but 99 percent, and I wondered how he could know that. Now this Methodist believes in hell, but I hope nobody's there. The way that radio evangelist talked, it sounded like they had a building program going on and he was taking reservations. He sounded happy about it! Who on earth could be happy about anyone being lost? Every soul lost is a defeat for our God—a personal defeat for Jesus Christ who bled on a cross that no one might be lost and that everyone might be saved.

I think about Mrs. Brown who was in her ninety-first year when she went to the hospital. She called me one morning with her voice full of excitement. I rushed out to the hospital. I said, "Mrs. Brown, what's happening?"

She said, "I want to tell you about a dream I had. I dreamed I was walking down the road; I came to a fork in the road and there was a man standing there—a beautiful man. I think he had to be Jesus. And when I got to the fork and didn't know which way to go, he said to me, 'Julia, you go to the right,' so I went to the right and I found the most wonderful people I've ever met in my life. It was like homecoming and Christmas all wrapped up into one and blown up ten times; it was beautiful! I know that was heaven."

And then she said, "But a strange thing happened. After he sent me to the right, he went to the left. Can you tell me anything about my dream?"

I asked, "Mrs. Brown, what do you think it means?"

She said, "I think it means I'm about to die, and the Lord was giving me some reassurance."

I said, "That may be."

And she said, "But the other thing that puzzles me is that after Jesus sent me to the right, he went to the left."

I said, "Mrs. Brown, I believe our Lord is the kind of Christ who doesn't just stand at the gates of heaven as a receiving committee, but runs a rescue shop outside the gates of hell. He stations himself across the gates of destruction so that if anyone is going inside they have to crawl over his outstretched body with their muddy boots."

She thought about it for a moment and then she smiled and said, "That would be just like Jesus, wouldn't it?" Eight days later the Lord came and took Mrs. Brown home.

I have thought about that dream many times. I believe the message of that dream is true. That's the kind of Christ we have. Does that mean, then, that you can wait as long as you want to repent of your sins and become a Christian? Does that mean you can live as you please, take personal freedom irresponsibly, interpret freedom to mean the right to do as you please? Can you just follow your own selfish dictates for ninety years and then finally come at last to repent of your sins and still be given a place in heaven? That's exactly what it means. What the old poet said was true when he declared, "Betwixt the stirrup and the ground mercy I asked, and mercy found" (William Camden, "Epitaph for a Man Killed by Falling from His Horse").

I believe you can capitalize on the compassion of Christ. You can put off your commitment to the last possible moment (if you know when that is), and if your commitment and your repentance are genuine and sincere, even at that eleventh hour, you'll be given a place in heaven. Like those laborers who sat around the square all day long, you can wait until the eleventh hour to go into the Lord's vineyard and when payday comes, you'll get the same pay as everybody else. I believe in deathbed repentance.

I also agree with Billy Sunday, who said that deathbed repentance is like burning the candle of life in the service of the devil and then blowing the smoke in God's face! I think you can burn the candle of life in the devil's service, blow the smoke in God's face, and then at the last moment accept him as your Lord and he'll give you a place with him in paradise. But, I think all of us are too decent to do that. I don't think anyone would want to do that to his best friend. Anyone who has ever come to the realization that he has already been wounded by our wickedness—he has already been nailed to a cross because of us—will not hurt him anymore. Because we can wait until the last possible moment, we *won't* wait until the last possible moment. We have too much decency to do that. We also need to see that those people who came in the eleventh hour to the vineyard missed the greater glory, because the greater glory was to be in that vineyard all day long. That's where you can find the roots of joy—the knowledge that you stood shoulder to shoulder with Christ, that you gave him the strength of your youth, that you offered yourself to him when you had a lot to give, that you were a co-laborer with Christ!

He is closer to you than you may have realized. He is the one who is knocking on the door to your heart. Have you ever listened for that special tapping?

The greatest danger comes from the fact that he does knock gently. There may come a time, although he persists in his knocking—keeps on knocking— there may come a time when we become so insensitive that we no longer hear it. We become acclimated to the sound of knocking.

My first assignment in the Methodist church was a little student appointment in Fleming, Georgia, just south of Savannah. I remember my first night in the little parsonage there. The little house was built almost in the bend of the Seaboard Coastline Railroad, and that was a busy railroad in those days. Those trains would come through there at a high rate of speed, making a lot of noise. I remember that first night how I was awakened by the sound of something that I thought was a thunderstorm approaching, thinking we were about to have some rain. I heard a little rumbling in the distance, and then it became louder and louder, and because it was continuous, I knew it wasn't a thunderstorm, but a train. Soon the shutters on the house started shaking and everything started trembling—dishes, furniture, etc. I was about to grab my wife by the arm and run for it. I thought the train had jumped the tracks and was going to plow right through our bedroom, when at the last possible moment it made that bend, and I heaved a sigh of relief.

A few weeks later, some friends came home with us from school. The next morning, when we all went in to breakfast, I noticed they had red, haggard eyes and faces, and they looked at me and asked, "How do you sleep with all that noise?" And I said, "What noise?" Something had happened to me during those weeks. The train had become an old friend and its noise, while never comforting, had blended into my routine.

That kind of thing can happen to our souls. The knocking of Jesus, which sounds so dramatic at first, if ignored, can be absorbed by the cacophony of routine. Do you remember when Paul was writing to Titus? He said some people have seared their consciences. They've known what was right, but they've done wrong, and they've set up such a conflict that their consciences have been seared and they are no longer responsive. It was like Felix, who, after hearing Paul preach, was moved by his message, but said, "Go away for the present; when I have an opportunity I will summon you" (Acts 24:25, RSV). Two years later Paul was still in his jail.

Is it any wonder, then, that the early church was always saying, "Behold, now is the acceptable time; behold, now is the day of salvation" (II Cor. 6:2*b*, RSV)? Our souls are like springs. How much flex is in them? That which we feel so strongly now, how can we be sure if we continue to ignore and delay, that it will still be there? We cannot know that. We cannot presume concerning a life and death matter. We must be responsive now.

Prior to coming to Texas, I was getting in touch with everything concerning my roots and who I am, gathering myself somehow for the challenge of this great church. I went one afternoon on a ride of more than two hundred fifty miles to the little church in Snipesville (with twenty-two members) where I had been baptized. I sat in a certain pew. I didn't just go to the altar where I was baptized. I sat in a pew where I had sat when I became a Christian and accepted the call to preach (all in one experience).

Now my call to the ministry had come months earlier. It had been a dramatic, mystical call experience, rather like the prophet Isaiah's call. I knew clearly out of that experience what God wanted me to do, but announcing to my father, telling my friends and the people I ran with that I was going to be a preacher was just too much to think about. And so I had rationalized my call, had put it away. I had worked harder in the church as my way of covering up my disobedience. I was president of the M.Y.F., and was doing all kinds of good works, but inside I knew I was a rebel. I was at cross-purposes with the man God wanted me to be. I put him off, rationalized, and delayed, and then finally one Sunday morning, things came to a head for me. I don't remember what the preacher said, but I know when I stood up for that last hymn I held onto the back of the pew with white knuckles. I felt that very moment that the train was leaving the station for me. I believed it was the last train, and if I didn't say yes then to the gentle tugging of Christ, I might not hear him anymore. But he was still there. He was there all of the time. He had been knocking until surely he must have gotten bloody knuckles. I realized that this is what his cross means. Is it not time that you responded, let him help you open the door that has been closed for so long?

# VII

## When Faith Grows Cold

*Four Steps Toward Renewing Your Faith*

What does a Christian do when his faith grows cold? How do you "rekindle the gift of God" when church work has become mechanical, when giving is done grudgingly, and when praying has become meaningless? Perhaps you can remember how his hand felt upon your life, but it has been a long time. Faith goes gradually, and we may not even be aware of its going.

Sam was a good man. He had grown up in the church. One of his earliest memories was of playing on a pallet behind the last pew in the small rural church near his home. Sam's family had always taken him to church; it had never been a case of insisting that the children "do as I say, not as I do." Sam's family had even included family prayers in their daily agenda. Sam could not remember a time when he did not believe in God.

When Sam grew up, went to college and moved away to the city, he did not consciously leave his faith behind. He sought out a church and went regularly for a time. Gradually, however, his business took him out of town more often and the weekends grew shorter and church became less important. The daily grind made it increasingly tough to give anything to daily devotions.

When Sam married and started his family, he made a feeble effort to do for his children what his parents had done for him in terms of a spiritual heritage, but it fell short. His wife did not have the same background in the church and believed that the weekend was "theirs" for good times with the family.

When I met Sam at the YMCA, he was ready to talk to a pastor. He knew he should feel fulfilled; after all, he had a good job and a fine family. However, he was empty inside, and it had been years since he felt like one of his infrequent prayers had gotten through. Something precious had dulled and almost died within Sam's soul, and he wanted to know how he could recover it.

In the last chapter we looked at the question of God's closeness to you. Indeed he still seeks you and has never given up on you. In spite of all of this, however, we find that our faith, like Sam's, is sometimes colder than we realized.

Some of us may have also shared the experience of Samson, who went out to flex his muscles against the Philistines, and did not even know that the Lord had left him. The Bible says, "He wist not that the Lord was departed from him" (Judg. 16:20, KJV). He had lost his great strength and did not even know it was gone until a great need arose and he reached down into the reservoir, only to find it empty. He did not know his reserves were gone until some high hour called for an expression of faith which he no longer had. Samson had become careless with his life. Those things that he had first shunned, he later tolerated, and that which he tolerated, he finally embraced. Someone has aptly said, "The little sins of a big man, if left unattended, become the big sins of a little man." Something had dulled and died inside Samson's soul, and he was not even aware that it was happening.

We never lose our faith all at once. Faith's fibers weaken slowly. Most of us are like Abraham's nephew, Lot. Had someone suggested to Lot that he move into the wicked city of Sodom, he would have been appalled at the suggestion. However, the Bible tells us Lot pitched his tent toward the plain, then in the valley, and finally we see him in the very gates of Sodom itself. I'm persuaded that it's the little compromises we make that erode our convictions and allow our faith to gradually weaken. The Bible declares that it's "the little foxes, that spoil the vines" (Song of Sol. 2:15, KJV). Not many of us have to contend with being swallowed by a large fish as Jonah was; however, most of us have felt the tug of the little minnows that nibble on us constantly.

If you have ever wondered about these minnows of life, it may help to begin by realizing that it does not help to blame the minnows. Blaming others will not help. The faith we lost gradually is a problem that is within ourselves and is not to be found within others. We cannot recapture the vitality of our faith by putting the blame for its disappearance on someone else or on our circumstances.

The other day in downtown Houston, I saw an interesting bumper sticker. It read, "Welcome back, Jesus!" When I saw that bumper sticker I remembered an old cartoon about an elderly couple driving down the road on Sunday afternoon. She's leaning against the door, and he is driving. They are impatient to get where they're going, but their progress is slowed dramatically by a cuddling young couple in the car before them who are in no hurry to get anywhere. Finding it impossible to pass, the elderly couple finally begin to strike up a conversation. The little old lady looks across at her husband, then looks at the couple in front of them, and asks her husband, "Why don't we sit together like that anymore?"

Quick as a flash, he responds, "I haven't moved."

God hasn't moved; Jesus hasn't gone anywhere! If we don't feel close to God anymore, we can be very certain that it is because something has occurred in our own souls. Jesus Christ is "the same yesterday, today, and forever." If our faith has grown cold, if we feel alone, if we feel apart from God, we can look within ourselves. This won't give us the total answer, but it does help to give us a realistic viewpoint. It helps us to get our life in a clearer focus.

If the prodigal had blamed his stuffy elder brother, as well he could have, if he had thought about his father with disdain and said, "He should have known better than to have given me all that money," he never would have gone home again. The Bible tells us the prodigal came to himself there, and assumed responsibility for getting up and going back to the father. You must assume personal responsibility for the coolness of your faith.

There is an old spiritual that declares, "Not my brother, nor my sister . . . not my father, nor my mother, but it's me, O Lord, standin' in the need of prayer." Until someone begins to take personal responsibility for what has happened to his or her own spiritual life, there is no way to help that person return to spiritual health.

All of us are encouraged when we remember that the problem of faith grown cold is not unique to any of us. Even the great ones in the Bible experienced faith problems. You'll recall that Abraham, who is the father of faith, once resorted to a cowardly lie to save his own skin. Abraham was down in Egypt when he realized that Pharaoh, who had a fondness for pretty women, was thinking of taking Sarah for himself. Abraham was so afraid that he might get in Pharaoh's way that he told the king that Sarah was his sister. David could write a beautiful psalm like "The Shepherd's Psalm," declaring: "Yea, though I walk through the valley of the shadow of death, I will fear no evil, for thou art with me." However, that same shepherd king could complain on another occasion, "How long, oh Lord, wilt thou hide thy face from me?" Simon Peter on one occasion could declare, "Thou art the Christ, the Son of the Living God," and in that declaration thrill not only his master, but the entire believing world. However, in a few short moments that same disciple could behave himself in such an unseemly manner that the Lord would say, "Get thee behind me, Satan." Even our Lord had a time in his life when he inquired of the heavens, "My God, my God, why has thou forsaken me?" (Matt. 27:46, KJV). You can comfort yourself with the knowledge that all people have struggled with the problem of faith grown cold. You are not unique in your need to "stir up the gift of God."

Now, having taken personal responsibility for the cooling of our faith, having been comforted by the realization that we are not alone in our struggle to "rekindle the gift of God that is within . . ." (II Tim. 1:6, RSV), the question still remains: How do we proceed? Let me suggest as a second step that we must get beyond ourselves. Paul suggested this to his younger friend Timothy when he urged him to rekindle his faith. The exhortation of Paul to Timothy had ministry as its objective. The gift of faith was not to be kept alive inside of Timothy simply to edify

Timothy's soul, or to create good feelings within himself. Faith was being given in order that it might be shared with others. Paul was reminding Timothy that God had entrusted a great deal to him, and he was to share it with others. We have a way of becoming like that we love, and when we love only ourselves and are preoccupied with selfish concerns, we become ill (Oswald W. S. McCall, *The Hand of God*). Spiritually, the springs of faith dry up within us. We cannot recover its vitality until we move beyond our own selfishness.

One of the most remarkable Christians I've ever known was a patient at the Cohen's Old Men's Home in Savannah, Georgia. He was an honorary member of the administrative board of a local Methodist church. As his new pastor, I went there with a host of others to ostensibly cheer him up. I discovered to my great surprise that this man, who was dreadfully crippled and had been confined to his room for more than ten years, was going to cheer me up. Richard Sconyers had the worst kind of arthritis; every bone in his body was practically frozen. He could not raise his hands off his lap. He could not wash himself, feed himself, shave himself. He was totally helpless. Each morning he was lifted into his wheelchair and then put back into his bed at night, and with the aid of eight pillows they tried to prepare him for sleep.

The first time I visited Mr. Sconyers I discovered that he had a ministry. He had learned that if someone would take a ballpoint pen and thread it through his crooked, disfigured fingers and then wrap tape around his entire hand and set a board across his knees, he could, by shifting his shoulder ever so slightly, write letters. With the discovery that he could write, Mr. Sconyers began to contact all the sick and lonely people he had heard about in the community and beyond—to point them to the saving help available in Jesus Christ. For many years he wrote between one hundred and one hundred twenty letters each month in a wonderful ministry of encouragement. Billy Graham heard about his ministry, wrote about him in his magazine, and mentioned him in a broadcast. The Sertoma Club of Savannah gave him its "Service to Mankind Award." Dozens of people from throughout the city came there to be lifted by the buoyancy of that man's spirit. All this, I thought, from a man who has to use the stick from an old window shade to fetch his handerchief or to wipe his eyes!

I never saw Richard Sconyers down for very long. I saw him have some bad days; I sat with him on the day of his wife's funeral because he was unable to attend. I saw tears in his eyes on several other occasions. However, he had a resiliency that never let him stay down long. I believe it was because his life was so centered in others.

Prior to leaving Savannah, I promised Mr. Sconyers that I would conduct his funeral. When the call came, I returned to that city and went to visit the old room from which he had carried on his ministry. His long-time nurse met me there and told me it was Mr. Sconyer's desire that I should have any one of his several modest possessions. I looked at the little air conditioner that a Sunday school class had given him. I looked at his little ten-inch black and white TV that some church friends had given him. I saw his old dog-eared Bible there on the bed beside where his chair would have sat. And then, I think I startled the nurse a little bit by requesting that she give me the old stick he used to fetch his handkerchief and his writing material. I wanted to hang that stick in my study so that it could remind me every single day of what God can do in the life of any person who sincerely wants to help others. The by-product of a ministry to others is a faith that will not grow cold.

If getting beyond yourself doesn't increase your faith, there is a third step: try something great for God. The Bible teaches us we were created for high adventure. Paul said, "God did not give us a spirit of timidity but a spirit of power and love and self-control" (II Tim. 3:7, RSV). Perhaps you need to demonstrate some of that power.

Jesus promised his disciples that when they were hauled in before the council for his sake, they were not to concern themselves about what they were supposed to say on such occasions. He told them he would be so close in that hour that they would know exactly what they were supposed to say. However, there is no promise in Scripture that when we retreat into a protective cover we will take his presence with us. God wants to keep us on the frontier. When the children of Israel looked toward the wilderness, they beheld the glory of God. The church sometimes suffers from a settling syndrome. We are always trying to get everything safely nailed down. There isn't much room for God within a safe church.

When Moses was leading the children of Israel toward the promised land, he was stopped by the Red Sea. Moses promised the people on that occasion that "The Lord will fight for you, and you have only to be still." However, you'll recall that the Lord thundered at Moses, inquiring, "Why do you cry to me? Tell the people of Israel to go forward" (Exod. 14:14-15, RSV).

And as they marched, the seas parted for them. Perhaps you need to try something great for God.

My home in South Georgia was not very far from Eatonton. Everyone in that section of the country is very familiar with the Uncle Remus stories. Our children were especially fond of hearing one of those stories having to do with "Brer Rabbit and the Witch Rabbit." If you recall that story, you know that Brer Rabbit was suffering from a dreadful malady called "mopes." (Many of us have a case of the mopes and don't know what's wrong with us!) Perhaps we would call it a good case of the blahs. At any rate, Brer Rabbit had heard that the Witch Rabbit down in the swamp could cure people of any kind of malady. He dragged himself down to the swamp and explained his problem to her. She promised him that she could indeed cure him, but first he would have to capture an elephant's tusk from a live elephant, a rattlesnake, a squirrel, and all kinds of bizarre things. The tasks to which she set him required all the resourcefulness that little rabbit had, and he had a great deal of it!

Now, somehow Brer Rabbit managed to get those things together and when he did, he returned to the swamp, and with a flourish, threw all the things she had requested at her feet and requested that she keep her promise and cure him of the mopes. The Witch Rabbit looked at the bounce in his step and the light in his eyes and said, "Brer Rabbit, you are cured!" Sometimes we get rid of the blahs by doing. We make a mistake to think we can pray all of our moods away. Some of them go only by action, not by praying. Now and again, we must pick ourselves up by the scruff of our spiritual necks and try something for God's sake.

Once I asked an engineer to come to a church I was serving to figure how much tonnage would be required to air-condition the sanctuary. I watched as he did a great deal of figuring, and then I saw him tear up the paper on which he had been writing and begin to figure anew. I inquired about the nature of his miscalculation. He said, "I was figuring this church like it was a theater." That aroused my curiosity, and I asked him about the difference between figuring for a theater and for a sanctuary. He said something to the effect that, "In a theater people become excited and with their excitement certain physiological changes occur in their bodies, such as increased heart rate, blood pressure, etc. These changes produce more heat. Consequently, you must figure on a higher level of tonnage." Then he began to say how it was in a church, and I stopped him! I didn't need or want to hear what he was about to say. He was going to say that in a church you could always count on people to be placid and unexcited. Perhaps that explains why we don't feel the presence of God beside us.

If none of the above suggestions helps in rekindling your faith, try walking in the light of remembered experiences. This is the fourth step or possibility. Many of us have a repository of faith from which we can draw. Timothy certainly had one. Paul reminded him of this when he said, "I am reminded of your sincere faith, a faith that dwelt first in your grand-mother Lois and your mother Eunice and now, I am sure, dwells in you" (II Tim. 1:5, RSV). He pointed Timothy to that special time in his life when Christian friends had placed their hands on him and prayed. Have you tried holding onto your high moments during those times when you are in the valley?

There is an old song which says, "If Satan says I don't have grace, I'll take him back to the start-ing place." In the *Pilgrim's Progress*, Hopeful and

Christian walk across an enchanted land, and Hopeful becomes so drowsy he has great difficulty staying awake. Christian keeps reminding him that they cannot sleep as others sleep, but must stay awake and be sober and alert. Hopeful asks how they can stay awake when they are so drowsy. Christian tells him, "We can have good discourse. Good discourse prevents drowsiness." Hopeful then inquires, "What kind of discourse? Where can we begin?" Christian says to him, "We can begin where God began with us. We can begin to recount the miracles of his mercy. We can recall his matchless grace." Sometimes our drowsiness is overcome only by the strong reminder of what it was like in the beginning.

I do not think it any geographical accident that during an especially trying time in his ministry, Jesus went back to the region along the Jordan where John at first baptized. Even for the Lord there were those times when he needed to return to the place where the heavens opened and "the spirit descended like a dove." Any experience in life that stimulates us to take a spiritual pilgrimage is a blessed experience.

Between my junior and senior years of college, I had a summer job with a telephone line crew along the coast of southeast Georgia. I was serving as a student pastor on the weekends, living in the parsonage, and during the weekdays working with a construction crew putting up telephone lines along the boggy marshes of the coast. That summer job was one of the most difficult I've ever experienced. All of the holes had to be dug by hand. You could not get equipment into those marshes. I can still recall the utter exhaustion I felt at the end of each long hot day. To make matters worse, the foreman of that crew didn't like me! I'm not exactly sure why he didn't like me, but for some reason there was almost instant dislike. I recall one afternoon when a sudden shower materialized, and I didn't want to ride on the back of an open truck for twenty miles. I saw that the foreman was alone in the cab of the truck, and thinking that perhaps I could ride with him there, I opened the door and started to climb inside. He took a long look at me and said, "Hinson, you are a member of the crew, and your place is on the back of the truck. Don't ever forget your place again." I climbed onto the back of the truck that afternoon, and during that twenty-mile ride when the heavens opened and I was totally drenched, I complained of everything God had ever done to me. I reminded God that I had not wanted to be a preacher to begin with—that had been my last choice. My father had told me I would starve to death, that it would be foolish to go into the ministry. I went through every difficulty I had experienced along the way leading toward my ordination. In fact, I made the grand mistake of going all the way back to a little grove of pine trees on a warm September night when I heard the voice of Christ calling me to be his man and to enter the Christian ministry. When I went back there, an old fire started to burn inside my soul. When I got off the truck, I tipped my soggy hat to the driver, because although I was cold on the outside, I had become very warm on the inside.

The apostle John said, "It was the tenth hour." He could remember every tree, every rock, every part of the scene. Paul declared, "It was at midday," when he first heard the voice from heaven. John Wesley declared, "It was a quarter before nine when I felt my heart strangely warmed." It was for them and is for us a blessed and never to be forgotten moment when we first heard the Lord. If your faith has lost its glow, perhaps you need to go back and recapture that moment. Stir up the gift of God that is within you.

If you have wondered how you can feel close to God, if you can know Christ on a personal basis, keep in mind the fact that you can play a part in making the relationship real. Could it be that the next step is actually up to you? Is the ball bouncing in your court? It is time for you to respond to the warmth of God's Spirit—to begin taking the steps that will renew your faith.

# VIII

## The Roots of Our Joy

### *Entering into Joy*

"I just want to have a little joy in my life." These words have been said to me many times. Quite often the one saying them is almost completely beaten down from some heavy burden or responsibility.

Sometimes this sense of a burden is not a single major problem. It may be several small but exasperating matters. Suddenly, the straw that broke the camel's back is added to our lives. We feel drained physically and emotionally.

Even though you may have a strong Christian faith you can feel emotionally drained. You may have discovered that God is closer to you than you have realized and that your faith in him is growing. However, you are still missing that desired sense of joy.

In this chapter I want to share with you some insights that may help you to find this joy for yourself. It will be helpful to begin with Jesus. Let us begin with his remarkable acceptance of people. In the eyes of a shrewd twentieth-century person, Jesus of Nazareth could be considered the greatest patsy who ever lived. He would have to be considered in that manner because he was used, incredibly used. Indeed, he was exploited even by those who should have loved him most—his own disciples. When he was on his way to Jerusalem, two of them came to him saying, "Grant us to sit, one at your right hand and one at your left, in your glory" (Mark 10:37, RSV), seeking to use their positions of closeness to gain prominence.

Jesus' healing of the ten lepers is another case. You will recall as the ten were miraculously cleansed and went on their way, only one of them returned to give thanks. Jesus inquired "Where are the other nine?" The wonder is not that Jesus healed. The wonder and, paradoxically, the secret to his joy, is that he kept on healing in the face of all the ingratitude he experienced.

From time to time he was forced to climb into the bow of a boat. He did this not in order to form some picturesque scene but to use the bow of a boat as his pulpit because the crush of the demanding multitude was so great. The crowds may actually have thrust him into the sea or done him bodily harm. Always the crowds came with their hands outstretched, never wishing to give anything, but always wanting something. Once his disciples heard him say, "Foxes have holes, and birds of the air have nests; but the Son of man has nowhere to lay his head" (Matt. 8:20, RSV).

Let us look at Jesus' life even further. Even the blind heard what manner of man he was. As Jesus passed through the town of Jericho, a blind man screamed at him saying, "Jesus, Son of David, have mercy on me!" (Luke 18:38, RSV). And the crowd, thinking Jesus had no time for the likes of blind Bartimaeus squatting in his rags beside the road, said, "Hush, man. He's on his way to die. He's about to divide history in half. Don't bother him now." But Bartimaeus kept on screaming, because he knew that if the rumors he had heard about this man were true, he could be stopped in his tracks by human need wherever and whenever he found that need. So he shouted again, "Jesus, Son of David, have mercy on me." This time Jesus heard him, stopped the processional, and gave the man his sight.

The demands were incessant. Jesus could not even die a demand-free death, for even as our Lord died on the cross, there was that one repentant thief beside him who screamed, "Don't die yet, Lord, save me!" Jesus was completely exploited, and yet we don't think of him as the victim of exploitation. Rather we consider him to be a great Savior. It is no small part of this that his finest and his most often repeated prayer was that the Father might use him, might get glory for himself through the ministry of his son.

Indeed, when Jesus looked for some way to summarize his ministry, and make it easy for us to remember, he chose very fittingly the common elements of bread and wine. Breaking the bread, he said, "This is my body broken for you." Pouring out the wine, he said, "This is my blood poured out for you."

We get closer to Jesus' secret of true joy in the portrait of the women of Jerusalem who came after him weeping and wailing. Jesus said, as he pointed a finger at them, "Do not weep for me" (Luke 23:28, RSV). He could have continued. "Weep for yourselves maybe. If you've never found anything exciting and compelling in your lives, if you've never discovered a mission for which you will lay down your lives, if you've never discovered anything so bracing and so gripping and so captivating as to cause you to lose your lives for the sake of that mission, then weep for yourselves." His joy was wholly related to his involvement in his Father's mission.

Jesus found his own source of joy in the glorification of his father, in the doing of his will. Because of this, we can admire him or we can reject him, but we cannot feel pity for him. Jesus even prayed that God would use him no matter if it involved the cross. Therefore, as he died they jeered him with the truth. They said, "He saved others; himself he cannot save" (Matt. 27:42, KJV). They were exactly right. It was not within the character of Jesus to save himself. There is very little in the gospels about Jesus' own joy in so many words. There is, however, a congruence with God's will. That is evident on practically every page. Is it too much to believe that this glorification of God was the source of a genuine sense of joy?

Bishop Arthur J. Moore was fond of saying, "Jesus never slept in a walled city." This man was accessible. He was available. He could be had, and he was had by both the rich and the poor. He was available to them all. I'm reminded of an expression we used in elementary school. When someone began to bully another, the courageous thing to say (in spite of the fact that you might be scared to death) was, "I'm like a turnip patch. You can have a mess of me any time you want it!" That's the way Jesus was. He was like a turnip patch. You could have a mess of him any time you wanted him. He was available.

Since Jesus clearly stated, "Where I am, there shall my servant be," what is our stance toward being used? I'm afraid that sometimes we have an imposition complex. Instead of praying every day of our lives that God might use us for his own glory, we are often afraid that we might be used. We are afraid that we might be used a trifle more than someone else is used, or perhaps if we are used, we might not get sufficient credit for all that we have done. Therefore, we become a little like a grain of wheat that refuses to fall into the earth (John 12:20ff.). It refuses to die unto itself, and as a result it doesn't bring forth much results. Caught up in our own desires we don't produce genuine results, and we don't experience much joy.

Now and again we wring our hands in exasperation, saying, "Why am I not more joyful? Why am I so unsatisfied? Why do I have so few real friends?" It could be that on the part of some of us there is an unwillingness to die. Perhaps we love our lives too much. We aren't willing to lay them down for Christ's sake. Maybe we're like the farmer, who, in the fall of the year when the atmospheric conditions are right, goes out to a field and drops a match into it and lets the stubble burn away. He isn't afraid of the fire going out of control, because before he dropped that match he had plowed a furrow around the field. It can burn only to a point and beyond that it cannot go.

A fellow named Pete guarded his own life that way. More than anything Pete had wanted to be a millionaire. Every member of his family, every friend, had helped to pay the price of Pete's all-consuming ambition.

He made his million and more! Having reached his monetary goal, however, he realized that something more urgent than money had been denied him. The more he accumulated of what he wanted, the less he wanted what he was accumulating.

Pete could tell you the number of days a new car smells new and how many steaks you can eat without getting fat. He had stuffed his pockets but starved his soul. Now he was wondering why his life was lacking in meaning and joy. "Isn't there more?" he asked.

When I first became a Christian, I was like the old ration coupons my parents told me about. I rationed myself out a little bit at a time. Each time I gave God a coupon, I waited expectantly for him to be impressed with my spirituality. I was amazed that he wasn't impressed at all. It was a traumatic experience for me to realize one day that he didn't want me to give him a coupon now and then. He wanted the entire book! My soul, I realized, he treats me like I'm bought and paid for. He acts as though he has written his name across my life and that he has every right to wring me out like a washcloth and leave me to dry. And then I remembered what Paul said: "I beseech you, brothers and sisters, that you present your bodies as a living sacrifice, holy and acceptable unto God, which is your spiritual (or your reasonable) service." It is God's expectation of you. I am persuaded that nothing really significant will happen in our hearts until we abandon our self-protecting ledgerkeeping attitudes toward life.

Do you remember the story of the talents? One man was given five, another given two, and finally one poor man received only one talent. (Most of us can identify with him.) Remember how the master eventually called for an accounting and the first two were blessed because they had multiplied theirs? Then there was that one man, with the one talent, who, when he presented his, there was all of that ugly talk about weeping and wailing in outer darkness and gnashing of teeth. Why do you think the master was angry? Was it because the man had tried and failed? Our Father knows how to handle failure. He can and does forgive us over and over again, gives us another chance, saying, "Risk it again for my sake." The one thing the master would not tolerate was the servant's refusal to try. He brought the talent back still wrapped in the original package! He had not bothered to risk or to try. It is no wonder that this attitude gives us no joy.

I remember a small boy who heard my second sermon. He sat on the front row in a little country church as I was trying to preach. All the while I was preaching, he was waving his bare feet to and fro and I was mesmerized by them. It was awful! After about five minutes of trying, I gave up. Following the benediction, the ten-year-old boy came up to me and said, "Brother Bill, would you come home with me and have dinner at our house?" And I thought, "He owes me that!" So I went with him, met his family, enjoyed a good dinner, then went back to South Georgia College where I was a student and forgot about it.

A couple of weeks later, I got a letter. When I pulled it out of my college mailbox, it rattled. I opened it, and out came fifty-seven cents in pennies, nickels, and dimes, and this letter from that boy: "Dear Brother Bill," the letter said, "I'm sending you my egg money to help you go to school to learn to be a better preacher." I thought it was the funniest thing. I remembered where I could reach his dad, and I called him. I said, "Look, I want to send it back. How do I send it back?" He said, "You can't. He never took better care of those chickens in his life. He's sending you every penny of his profit. He's going to keep on sending you his profit, and if you send it back you'll break his heart."

The next week there was another gift, and the next, and the months became years. There came a time when I didn't laugh any more upon receiving his letter, but I'd go back to my room, get on my knees and pray, "Oh, God help me to be worthy of that little boy's sacrifice." Suddenly C's weren't good enough, and just getting by didn't satisfy me anymore.

Somebody was laying everything down for me, and I had no choice but to accept it. I couldn't do anything about it except respond to it.

These are the people who move the world for Christ's sake. You and I are not called to be successes, not called to be super people, not called to have all of the answers. There is no joy for you in those directions. You and I are called to be servant people. We were created to be fulfilled only by serving as Christ served, giving ourselves in service to the world for Christ's sake.

I read a story in one of Howard Thurman's books that I also remember hearing him tell. It was about himself when he was a child. He and a group of little boys were walking across a sandlot one day, and they saw some larger boys playing baseball there. Little Howard, wanting to impress his friends, said, "Hey, I'll bet I could get an 'uppance,' a chance at bat, with those boys." They said, "Oh, go on, Howard, they won't let a little kid like you have a turn at bat." But little Howard had an ace up his sleeve. He recognized one of those big boys as someone who was dating his oldest sister, and he knew that boy would do anything to get in good with the family. So, Howard waited until that boy was about to bat, then he tugged at his sleeve and asked for his uppance. The boy started to give him a knuckle sandwich, then saw who it was and said, "Sure, Howard, you can have my bat." Howard choked up on the bat, stepped in the batter's box and the pitcher threw a fast ball that was in the mitt before he got his bat around! It was strike one, and then it was strike two, and then strike three, and he was out almost before he had gotten there.

Howard Thurman said, "I didn't hit a home run; I didn't even get a foul tip; but when I walked back to my little group of friends, I was so very proud because I'd stood in the batter's box. I'd had my uppance and I'd taken my cuts."

I believe in the final analysis the roots of our joy can be found in the knowledge that we stood in the batter's box in our day, and in our time, and that we swung from the heels! We gave it everything we had. We took our cuts for Christ's sake in the time in which we lived.

The saddest part of Jesus' story about the laborers in the vineyard is not only that those who had been there all day long begrudged God's generosity in paying the latecomers the same wages, but that they failed to see the additional glory, the additional source of joy that had been given to them. They had enjoyed the privilege of being in that vineyard throughout the long day! They had been given a place to serve, a chance to be a "co-laborer with Christ," to be one with him who declared, "My Father works and I work too."

During the years just after the turn of the century, Sam Jones was a great evangelist. Walt Holcomb, his son-in-law, preached in one of my churches once, and I remember one of his favorite stories that is also one of mine. He told how Sam Jones closed one of his revival services, saying to the congregation, "If we could compare the kingdom of God to a locomotive, what part would you like to be?" Someone raised his hand and said, "Brother Jones, I'd like to be the whistle and sound God's praises." Somebody else raised his hand and said, "I'd like to be the wheel and just roll down the track." Brother Jones wasn't very impressed with the responses until finally a timid soul down near the front raised his hand and said, "Brother Jones, I'd like to be the black coal and just burn myself up for Christ's sake!" Sam Jones swallowed hard and said, "Brothers and sisters, we have enough whistles and wheels in the church now. We need more coal." We need more people who are willing to be burned up for Christ's sake.

We must choose whether we are here to save our lives or to give our lives in service to the world for Christ's sake. The necessity of making that choice was brought home to me dramatically in the circumstances surrounding my father's death. I was a senior in seminary at the time Daddy died. He had suffered a stroke and a heart attack some two weeks earlier, but we had been assured by his physician that he was steadily improving. After a short visit, my wife and I had returned to Emory where I was to take my final examinations. However, on that fourteenth day, my father experienced his final heart attack.

My little sister, Ann, was the only family member present in the room when Daddy's chest pains began. My mother and some of the rest of the family had gone around to my brother's home for a short rest. When the pains began, Daddy raised the one hand not immobilized by his stroke and said to my sister, "Go get Bill, and ask him to hold my hand and help the hurt." Ann explained to Daddy that she couldn't go get me because I was more than two hundred miles away at the time. However, he repeated his request, and it was then that she realized what was happening, and she ran to get the doctor and the nurses. They worked feverishly over him, but couldn't save him. I was unable to get to him before he died. I wrecked a car trying to get there, but I didn't make it.

When I arrived in Jessup, Georgia, my sister, Ann, told me about my father's request. She explained how he had raised his hand just prior to his death, and had asked her to go get me. When she told me about that,

I was overwhelmed by a feeling of self-pity. I said, "Oh, God, I would have given ten years of my life to have made it here in time to hold that hand!" For a long time I failed to see any deeper meanings in that sad request. However, after a time, God helped me move beyond my self-pity to the realization that as long as I live if I have "eyes to see" and "ears to hear," there will be people all around me holding up their hands asking me to hold them and to help the hurt. And I had to decide whether I was going to go through life holding hands with myself or reaching out to help the hurt of the world.

You must decide; all of us must make that decision. For my part, I have elected to follow that gentle man, who, when his soul was deeply troubled, raised the question, "What shall I say then? Father, save me from this hour! No! For this cause came I to this hour. Use me to glorify thy name." That is the only source of joy.

# IX

# Just a Bunch of Builders

## *From Hindrance to Helper*

From the beginning, his parents had put him down.
He was old enough to spread his wings, but his
parents kept clipping them. When Sam flunked out of
a state college, his parents said his grades confirmed
what they'd known all along. They suggested the
army, but they didn't really believe anything could
help him.

A church college agreed to give him another chance.
Shortly after his first successful semester, Sam felt
called into the ministry. When he told his mother, she
suggested that they go visit his closet. She showed
him his old beach ball, his tennis racket, his football,
and said, "You've never been good at anything, never
finished anything you started. The ministry won't be
any different."

We all know how close the church also came to
losing Saul of Tarsus, because when he tried to
become a preacher of the gospel, there were those
who wouldn't let him forget what he had been. And it
was Barnabas—thank God for Barnabas—who put his
arm around his shoulder one day and said, "Look, I
believe in this man Paul. I trust him. He's my friend. I
think we ought to receive him with open arms and
hearts." He sponsored him when all others suspected.

I think, when Paul was talking about all the things Christians have going for them, he remembered the Son of Encouragement with whom he shared so much of his life, and he said we ought to encourage one another; we ought to believe in each other; we ought to build one another up (I Thess. 5:1ff).

Even Jesus, who lived so close to God, needed to be appreciated. Do you remember when he healed the ten lepers? As they went on their way to see the priest, they were miraculously cleansed, but only one of them returned to give thanks to their great benefactor. Jesus looked at that one and inquired in a plaintive tone, "Where are the other nine? Where is the thanksgiving? Where is the appreciation, the gratitude for what I have done?"

When Jesus went to the Garden of Gethsemane, he was looking for encouragement from the Father and from his friends. He received encouragement from the Father, but his friends disappointed him. And if the only begotten Son of God needed encouragement, think how much more all of us need it.

In the biography of Henry Ford, the multimillionaire, we read about the discovery of a rather strange object in his workshop. Shortly after his death they found an old shoe box beneath his workbench. When they opened the box, they found, of all things, a tiny test tube and these words written on the tape, "Thomas Edison's last breath." Everyone who knew Henry Ford knew why he had that test tube with the mythical breath beneath his bench. When he first advanced the idea of a gasoline engine, an automobile, there were those who scoffed and mocked, saying, "It will never go. You can't make that thing run." However, Henry Ford went to a banquet one evening at which Thomas Edison, already a renowned inventor, was speaking. No one knows quite how it happened. Perhaps Henry Ford began to tell him about his idea, and maybe even sketched an outline of his thinking on a napkin. No one knows precisely what occurred, but sometime during that evening, Thomas Edison said to Henry Ford, "I believe it'll work. Why don't you go build it?" And on the strength of that, though no one else believed, Henry Ford found the courage to persist and to carry out his ambition.

The path of faith includes giving ourselves whole-heartedly to Christ. This then becomes quite specific in giving to others. Helping others begins with encouraging them and building them up. Jesus always looked for the best in people. He always spoke to the best. He was a believer in that old proverb, "There is a king (or queen) in every person. Speak to the king and the king will come out." He looked at Levi and saw Matthew. He was always seeing people with a double vision—what they were and what they could become. He was willing to risk the hostility of an entire city to speak to Zacchaeus. He invited himself to that man's home to have dinner, to have conversation. He spoke to the man to whom no one else would speak. He was willing to risk the unpopularity in order that he might say to Zacchaeus, "Hey, man, you're a child of Abraham, too. Maybe you've forgotten that for a little while, but you really are important."

The harshest words Jesus spoke were reserved for those people who were always seeing the splinters in their brothers' and sisters' eyes and were never aware of the two-by-fours in their own eyes. Jesus mocked such people. He ridiculed such individuals. And you and I know what he was talking about.

I think about Roy, who kept the health club at the

YMCA to which I belonged. I suppose he still does. Roy did his job well. He mopped out the shower stalls, kept the place meticulously clean, saw that our shorts and our socks were washed and put back in our lockers, and when he wasn't working at the health club, was out running. Roy ran ten and twelve miles a day, and each time there was a road race he always entered. Finally Roy placed. One day I walked into the health club, and Roy met me at the door with a tiny trophy in his hand. He held it up, grinning from ear to ear, saying, "Bill, look! I won third place."

And I said, "Roy, that's terrific!" I knew it was probably the first trophy he'd ever won in his life. He was inordinately proud, and I was proud of him. After I told him so, I walked over to my locker and started to get dressed. Some other guys walked in and he made the same little speech. But, several of the fellows started to tease him. They said, "What's the matter with you, Roy? Why did you take third place? Why didn't you win first place?" And I know those guys. I know that they didn't mean to hurt him, but as I listened to them tease, I thought, this is the worst kind of sin there is, a sin against the spirit.

I grew up in a church believing that if I didn't "drink, smoke, or chew, or run around with girls who do," I'd be a good little boy. I thought you defined goodness in terms of all the things you didn't do, and I thought the worst sins were the sins of the flesh. I was grown before I realized that the worst sins are not the sins of the flesh; our Lord quickly and easily forgives us those sins when we repent of them. The worst sins are the sins against the spirit. When someone looks at another individual who's doing his or her dead-level best and they say it isn't good enough, that's the worst kind of sin. That's the sin against the spirit of a person.

You can leave all that behind. If you have regularly put people down, Christ's closeness will help you to turn from that and begin to build people up. It can even start with very small things.

I remember one Sunday morning when Jean and I were vacationing on the West Coast. We went to church in San Jose and then drove north to get to Sausalito before the sailboat races that afternoon. We'd heard about that beautiful scenery, and we wanted to see the colorful race. So we got a reservation in a restaurant out over the bay and watched the magnificent procession of boats as they came by where we were seated. We enjoyed the afternoon thoroughly, and after it was over we left our table and went out into the lobby to pay the check. While I was waiting my turn in line at the cash register, I admired all of the beautiful plants in the lobby. There were some gorgeous ones, including a corn plant that stretched all the way to the ceiling. While I was admiring it, a lady brushed past me, almost knocked me over in her eagerness to get at that plant which had one leaf beginning to turn yellow at the bottom of it, a very normal thing for that plant. She rushed over and snatched that yellowing leaf away, muttering to her companion, "That yellow leaf just spoils the whole thing for me." I remember thinking as I walked to the cash register, "Sister, I'm so glad you live in California!"

People with jaundiced eyes make me tired. They look at something, and they don't see its beauty because they have eyes only for the yellow leaves. They look at others, and they don't see all the good, the beauty, and the struggle to do what's right and honorable and true. They see only that one thing others aren't doing. People with jaundiced eyes are almost like vultures who sail over beautiful valleys

103

and instead of seeing any of the lush beauty, they see only that for which their eye is trained, the rotten and the ugly and the decaying. I tell you, it is a hurting thing to be around folk who are always playing district attorney. They are real hindrances to anyone's joy.

The problem with all of this is that sometimes all of us are prone to make snap judgments. We see others and come to a conclusion that is unmerited and even go so far as to discourage them. I remember doing that myself. I recall when Beth Hayworth first called me and told me she wanted to get married. She asked me about a certain date on the calendar. I checked and saw that it was open. She said, "Will you officiate?" I said, "Certainly, but it is customary for me to counsel persons before I officiate, so you'll have to bring that fellow you're going to marry in to see me." I knew she was going to marry a skinny kid from Texas, who was still in college, and I wanted to talk to him.

They came into my office and I did my usual counseling, and then I asked that young man what he was going to do for a living when he got out of college. I reminded him that Beth was accustomed to a rather good life. She came from a substantial family. She had never suffered, nor wanted for anything. "How do you propose to take care of this beautiful girl who's grown up in our church?" I asked. And he looked me straight in the eye and said, "I'm going to be a professional golfer. I'm going to get on the tour and make a lot of money." And I said, "You and five hundred thousand more! You'd better wake up, man. You'd better learn how to do something else so you can make a living for this girl. I don't want you to bring her back and have her parents feed her, and clothe her and take care of her. You ought to make some definite plans about how you can make a living for your wife."

The next time I saw Bill Rogers, he was playing in the Master's. I tried to talk to him, but he wasn't very friendly to me, and I can't blame him. The first year that guy was on the tour he made two hundred thousand dollars. And I just looked at that young man who said he wanted to be a professional golfer and decided he didn't have what it takes. It is a horrible thing when we do that to each other. I have suffered myself from people like that.

When I first went into the ministry, I found myself on my own—no help for school. My mother had been listening to a big radio preacher. She said, "I heard that man preach. He cares about people. If you'll go see him, he'll help you get in school. He'll find a way to get you in college." I was reluctant to go by myself, so I found three other ministerial students, and the four of us got an appointment with that preacher, and we went down to talk to him about helping us go to school. I'll remember it the rest of my life. He talked to us all and then asked me to stay when the others were gone. He said to me as gently, but firmly, as he could, "Look, Bill, I don't think you can make it. I know you're a graduate of Snipesville Academy; I know where you come from. I am not sure you're college material. And I especially don't think you can go on to seminary."

I never believed him, but in the dark nights of my soul when things weren't going well for me and I was discouraged, I sometimes let fear creep into my mind . . . maybe he knew what he was talking about . . . maybe I don't have it.

One of the worst things we can do to others is to make them doubt themselves. That is a terrible thing, because the success of our mission in life is largely dependent, not only upon what faith we have in ourselves, but upon what faith other people have in us. "Oh," you say, "I'm not like that. I wouldn't put anybody down." I'm not so sure. I know about a man whose soul is scarred this very day. He's in his sixties now. He was the last of a large family. All of his life his father had wanted a son, but they kept on having daughters. Finally, he had a son. He wanted a son because he had been a great athlete and he was determined that his son would be an even greater athlete, but the boy turned out to be one of those delightful creatures who can't walk and chew gum at the same time—I mean totally uncoordinated . . . couldn't catch a fly ball if it had biscuits for wheels. I mean, he just couldn't do it.

One day when he was Little League age, his father was hitting him some grounders and the boy was trying to catch them and he couldn't. And finally, his dad gave up, threw down the bat, turned to his son and said, "All of my life I wanted a son, and I got you." And that boy has never gotten over it. As long as he lives, he will be scarred because he didn't get approval and acceptance from his father. What he got was hindrance from one who could have been his helper.

Young people come into my office and through their tears they say to me, "Pastor, I have never received an unqualified compliment from my parents. If I make all A's on my report card and one B, they don't commend me for the A's. They say, 'Why did you make that B?' If I cut the grass as best I can, they say, 'You did all right in the front, but you left some around the garbage can in back.' If I wash the car, they'll say, 'What about that whitewall tire you didn't get clean?' I can never remember my parents giving me an unqualified compliment. They always say 'but' or 'however.' They always put a hook in. How can I please my parents? I can't comb my hair; I can't dress; I can't do anything to please them." It always scares me to death when I hear that because children have a way of living up to or down to our expectations of them. Ian Maclaren has said, "Be kind. Everyone's fighting a hard battle." The Bible says, "Be kind to one another, tenderhearted, forgiving one another" (Eph. 4:32, RSV).

I remember my last class reunion. I always get depressed when we have those class reunions because everyone else seems to be getting older; it gets me down. And then I'm depressed for several other reasons. The menu is always the same. We always have that clammy kind of potato salad with too many onions, and we have those garden peas that are the big, wrinkled, chinaberry kind, and they're hard—they crack when you bite them. And we always have ham sliced so thin it only has one side and it crumples in your plate, and they always charge a large amount for it. And then I don't like those reunions because the agenda never varies. We stand up one after the other and tell how long we've been married to the same person and what wonderful things our children are doing. It's so boring because you have to wait while they talk about their ordinary children until it's your turn to tell them about your truly remarkable children!

Last reunion, as I was sitting there waiting for my turn, one woman got up and went into the next room. She sat down at the bar and ordered a double. And when she did, my end of the room went wild. "The very nerve, the audacity of that woman! Who does she think she is?" I decided I wanted to talk with her, so I went in, sat down beside her and ordered a Tab on the rocks. After she got over the fact that I had become a preacher and that I would come into the bar to talk with her, she laid it on me.

She said, "Bill, do you remember my husband?"

I said, "Of course I do—we went through school together. You married soon after graduation, didn't you?"

She said, "We did; we loved each other all our lives. Several years ago, he drowned during a storm on the gulf."

I said, "I'm so sorry."

Then she said, "We had a beautiful daughter, nineteen years old. Last year she went to her room, took a pistol out of the drawer, and killed herself."

She couldn't brag about her husband! She couldn't tell about the daughter she didn't have!

She said, "I'm drinking this stuff and trying to keep on putting one foot in front of the other."

And I thought about that old verse which says, "Lord, give me eyes lest I, as people will, should pass by somebody else's Calvary and call it just a hill." Everybody's fighting a hard battle. That is why the Bible instructs us to be kind, tenderhearted, and forgiving.

What do all these stories mean? I have recounted some stories to you. Some of them you may have known, such as the ones about Jesus and Saul. The others may be new to you—the ones about Henry Ford and Thomas Edison; Roy the attendant at the health club; the woman in Sausalito with the yellow leaf; Sam, who felt called to the ministry; Beth Hayworth and Bill Rogers and the others—all of these stories are to make a point.

I want to show you that you are desperately needed. Let me tell you one additional story. I had a chance to go to the Masters tournament one year. (I always hasten to tell my golfing friends not to play in it—to be a spectator.) I decided I wanted to do what so many others do. I wanted to be a part of Arnold's army. I know Arnold doesn't win much anymore; I know he has the "yips" with his putter. He also has the problem many of us have . . . when he hits the ball he has a lot of postage on it, but no clear address—he doesn't always know where it is going. I knew he wouldn't win, but he still has charisma, charm, and I wanted to walk with his army around that course— that beautiful course in Augusta. We had not gone very far before he yanked one down in the edge of the creek. I watched as he tried to figure out what to do. I looked at the man beside me, figured he didn't know as much about golf as I do, so I thought I'd describe Arnold's dilemma. I said, "Now Arnold's problem is he has to hit a two iron to get it out of the edge of that water, but if he hits it hard it will go all the way across the fairway. He'll be out-of-bounds and that's a two-stroke penalty. Arnold is in a real bind."

That fellow looked at me like I didn't know anything and asked, "Fellow, is this your first time at the Masters?"

I said, "Yes sir."

He said, "If you'd ever been here before, you would know Arnold's not in trouble. He's going to hit the ball hard, but he won't hit it out-of-bounds. He'll hit it toward the crowd."

And I watched him. He did hit it with a long iron. He hit it hard, and it went straight toward the crowd and someone in that crowd who loved him a lot more than I did got in front of that ball and let it hit him! And when the ball finished bouncing around and they finished kicking it, it was right back on the fairway! And then that man looked at me as he shook his head and said, "As long as there's a crowd at Augusta National, Arnold Palmer will never hit it out-of-bounds."

You are needed to be a helper for so many people. Apart from you, some will go out of life's bounds and may stay there. One of the great compensations of life has to do with your own growth as you respond to the needs of other people. Your joy will begin to grow as you accept this calling from the Christ that you have let into your heart. Listen for the calling and become a helper, that your joy may become full. If you have been a hindrance to others in the past, consider how much it will mean for you to become a helper.

# X

# When Will the World Believe?

*Someone Has to Make It Real*

One of the things that hurts us most is to see someone who has been lifted up in the eye of the public come crashing down. Whether it be an ex-president, some other politician, or anyone in the world who is called great, when they are exposed and censured, when their clay feet are revealed, it hurts us. Indeed, when people begin to probe at those whom we admire and respect, we would just as soon they stop the probe, because all the time, we are hoping that nothing ugly is exposed about that person. We all have an inherent need to respect and admire and look up to people. We have a need for models.

There is, however, something much more important than even being a perfect model. None of us need perfect models, and I'm grateful for that. A long time before modern psychology told us that even the finest among us have conflicts and ambiguities, the Bible said all of us are sinners and if we say we don't have any sin, we aren't telling the truth. We understand that it is too late to talk about innocence for most of us. Even when we try, we are less than perfect models. We know in our honest moments we aren't snow-white. We are called to the impossible possibility. We understand, and we are trying to accept our struggles and our ambiguities.

I think about that field goal kicker who played for the Atlanta Falcons—maybe he still does. I remember one of the games I was watching when in the last few seconds, he had an opportunity to win the game. He missed. I think they called it "wide right." In the postgame show, when everyone was so depressed about it, a sports reporter interviewed the kicker and asked him what in the world happened. He said, "I don't know. I had a perfect snap from center. I got a perfect hold. I made a perfect kick, but the ball didn't go through the uprights." He steadfastly held to his story, and I thought, this is ridiculous! The ball missed the goal; it didn't go through the uprights, and there he is saying, "I did everything perfectly."

You do not have to worry about this kind of perfection. However, that may be a barrier that is holding you back from further growth as a Christian. You may be worried about *inner* perfection. Many people are. Some are worried about *outer* perfection, a righteousness of their own actions before God. It is almost imperative that you discover that you can make mistakes as a Christian and be forgiven and still be led by God. We can go on and say, "Hey, I missed it. I really messed up." We can know that we're all right even when we mess up. We have a God who accepts us and loves us and offers grace that puts us on our feet and keeps us going.

Can I really try to help others and accept it when I fail? You certainly can. In this chapter I want to help you to discover that you can dare to help people even if you are aware that you sometimes fail. I want you to come to know that we have a commitment to something big out there. We're in the grips of it, and we're pressing on. When we mess up we know we've messed up, but we're determined to get back on our feet. Because of God's grace, we can't wait to get up and give it another go.

I think that's the kind of modeling the world is after. And that is the kind of modeling that helps the most. We don't need any more phonies. You never feel good when you think that influence requires perfection. It doesn't. You don't have to worry about that anymore. You can become, however, a person who makes a great impact. Influence that is well-intended although imperfect can still be powerful and have far-reaching effects.

You may not realize how great your influence on others can become. Most of us are relatively blind to the power of our influence at first. I remember reading about the great English preacher, who, in his early years, had peddled pornography, the worst kind of filth. He had gained his livelihood from it, and later, when he was converted to Christ and became a preacher of the gospel, was given over to deep bouts of depression. At the heart of his depression was the remorse of all of his wasted influence, the bad influence he had been on the youth and people around him. He wept over wasted influence. Your capacity to influence others may be far greater than you realize at this time.

I tell you, influence is powerful. Sometimes it seems almost irrevocable. Consider Simon Peter, who, when Jesus was crucified, should have pulled the group together. He was the leader; he was supposed to be the strong one. He should have waited in obedience to the command of the Lord, but do you remember what he did? He became sick to his stomach with lost hopes and blasted dreams. He turned to that little band and said, "I'm going fishing." And the worst part about his declaration that he was going back to the boats was that he carried most of that little band with him! He had to live with that. He had to live with the fact that he had not only gone fishing, but he'd carried some other people with him, too.

Throughout the ministry of Paul, you see him reminding himself that he persecuted the church at one time, that not only did he persecute the church, but that he stood there holding the coats of people while they stoned Stephen to death. He didn't throw the stones, but he was keeper of the coats! He had made it possible for other people to throw stones, and that's equally as bad. Influence is a strong and powerful thing; we all have the capacity to shape the lives of others more than we realize. In fact, our greatest capacity to inspire others is simply that we don't fit any of the perfect stereotypes.

Alan was a high school jock—a three-letter man in football, baseball, and basketball. He was not a Christian and couldn't understand why he kept having thoughts about the ministry. Such thoughts were consistently shelved by Alan because he could not visualize himself as a pastor. What he had observed in many sermon-pushers left him cold.

One day Alan was pitching in an unofficial baseball game when the newly appointed pastor of his church appeared. After watching for several innings, the pastor requested a couple of swings. The boys obliged, and Alan threw the pastor an easy one, which he hit out of the ballpark. Then Alan threw him his best fast-ball and his best curve, and the park wouldn't hold them.

When the game was over, the pastor invited Alan to a game of golf. There was still no sermon, no mention of church. Alan went home to try to piece together his shattered stereotype of preachers.

One of the saddest things to read in the Bible is in the Book of Romans when Paul said, "The name of God is blasphemed among the Gentiles because of you" (Rom. 2:24, RSV). That's about the worst thing I know. And about the best thing I know is in the story of Ruth and Naomi. When Ruth had lived with Naomi for a time, she said, "I want to worship your God." I want a good dose of your religion. I want to bow down before your altar. I want to be with you, because I see in you all that I need to make life exciting, and meaningful, and purposeful. Wow! Is that influence something! It's like throwing a stone into a pond and the ripples starting out and your not being able to retrieve those ripples. Whether they're good or bad, they keep on going. Your influence is like that. Once it gets started you cannot bring it back again.

We are the embodiment of something or someone. No one is moved or influenced by an abstraction. Maybe an artist can get into an abstract painting, or a few of us can appreciate those things, but no one is changed by an abstraction. Take the word *courage* for instance. It was only a word for many until the winter a plane went down in an icy river in Washington, D.C. One man clung to the tail section of that broken plane, and when a helicopter lowered a preserver, he handed it first to one and then to another fellow passenger, until finally he was no longer there to save anyone, for he had gone beneath the icy waves. Everybody wanted to know him. They wanted to know his name —they wanted to know where he was from, wanted to know about his family, his parents, his friends—because suddenly *courage* was no longer a word, it was wrapped up in flesh, and for a little while the world saw courage and was enthralled and moved by it.

You and I embody something. We're setting some kind of an example. Even children have this great capability. There is a little boy in Albany, Georgia, who is a special friend of mine. He must be about five now. He came to my study one day. His mother had called for an appointment. He came with a momentous declaration and announcement. He had finally been given the kitten of his dreams, just a little furry thing, and he wanted to see his pastor because he wanted to tell me, as he looked me steadily in the eye, "Pastor, I have named my kitten Dr. Hinson." I can't get away from that! I've come to terms with the fact that something very important to this little guy bears my name. That means I have a place in his constellation. Somewhere in his stars I have a place. I am one of them, and I need to shine brightly for him because I'm an important person in his life. I feel that burden, and who among us would not?

I remember an experience when my son was in junior high. We were out in front of the parsonage one afternoon playing basketball. We've had lots of great games, he and I. We were having one of our better games, but the phone kept ringing, and it was a girl who wanted to be his steady girlfriend. Remember those "going steady" days in the seventh grade? And he'd go and talk for a moment and hang up, and she'd call back again. He was exasperated because Dad wanted to give him a couple of hours, and she kept interrupting. Finally, the conversation went sour and he said, "Look, I don't want to be your boyfriend. I don't want to go steady with you."

When the girl said an ugly word, he said, "And

that's another thing I don't like about you. You have a dirty mouth."

And she said, "John, don't you know everybody in our class talks like that but you?"

And he said, "That's all right; my daddy doesn't talk like that, and until I hear him talk like that, I'm not going to talk like that either."

As soon as I had a few moments, I found a private place of prayer, and I made a commitment to a son who by now has heard every kind of language there is. I know that, but I made a commitment that morning that even though he'd hear all that, he'd never hear it from his daddy.

I think the world is waiting for Christians to set an example in their speech, in their conduct, in their faith, in their love, and in their purity. I believe the world is waiting to see us embody these qualities and show the world that our faith is, indeed, an incarnational faith. The only claim to fame we have, the only distinctiveness which sets us apart from the other religions, is that in Christianity we see the incursion of Almighty God into human life. We see God revealed in a person, and if we don't see God revealed in the lives of the people who are named by his name, then we can't expect the world to believe.

Somebody said something to me the other day about Vidalia onions. I wish I'd brought a truckload with me from Georgia because I find people in Texas like Vidalia onions. Well, you might be interested to know that there is a little community about a hundred miles from Vidalia that had a lawsuit on its hands because some ambitious entrepreneur came up with the idea of selling his onions as Vidalia onions. He didn't live in Vidalia, but he put up a sign—a big sign—that said "Vidalia," and then in little letters,

"-type onions for sale." And the folk in Vidalia didn't take kindly to that. They didn't think people ought to sell "Vidalia-type" onions. Either it's a Vidalia onion, or it isn't.

The world is rightfully very discriminating and is watching to see whether or not Christians show some stability even in a shattered world like ours. You probably haven't had anyone come up to you and say to you, "What do you believe about God? How is he real to you? I want to get what you have." However, there are many people who feel lost. There are many who are looking for someone in whom they can believe. They don't need a perfect example, but they are in search of something that will help them as it has helped you. We have sophisticated shoppers. We have auditors, if you please, who want to judge us in our recreation time. They want to judge us at work. They want to get a good idea of how our convictions stand up under the ordinary processes of life. That's what the world is looking for in us more than special signs or great success stories. They want something with substance that goes beyond the superficial. They want a friend who can introduce them to that someone who will become their divine friend.

Did you read about that tree that is growing in a little village in Alabama? This tree was covered over with a kudzu vine. One day somebody drove past that tree, looked into the sunset, and the resulting silhouette looked for all the world like Jesus. And the people got so excited they came for hundreds of miles around and had services there and shouted hallelujah—praise the Lord—he's about to come back again! Look at that tree at sundown and you can see a silhouette—you can see a shadow of Jesus. And it made me kind of sick, because I don't think the world needs shadows.

I think the world's waiting for soldiers. I don't think the world wants to see a tree that looks like Jesus at sundown. I believe the world wants to see people who bear a strong family resemblance to Christ in the daytime—people who earn their salaries—people who pay their bills—people who keep their word—people who can be counted on to be kind even if they aren't always correct—people who love so much that it makes them sick when they hurt somebody else. That is the way that you can help the most in this world.

Undoubtedly, you have read about the Shroud of Turin. It is in many ways a remarkable story. Scientists are testing a piece of linen cloth to see if it can be the cloth that was wrapped around the body of our crucified Savior. There are busloads of people going to see that thing. I think that's all right, but I think it's infinitely more important not just to determine where the body of Jesus might have been. I think it's even more important to determine where his body of followers is now and to become part of them.

Ours is an incarnational faith. The Bible tells us, "In those days Peter stood up among the brethren" (Acts 1:15, RSV). Isn't it a wonderful thing when someone stands up in the place where you live and work; when someone starts to fly his colors and to raise the mantle of Christ, and says, "Hey, I'm one of his and I'm willing to take the burden of being in the spotlight—of being misunderstood. I'm willing to have people point the finger at me. I don't want to hide behind flimsy excuses anymore." You know, it's something to be in the spotlight.

The problem is that without realizing it we often become hypocrites in reverse. We do not want to admit all that we really believe about God. We don't

119

want to stand in the spotlight. We sometimes want to come off as being worse than we really are because we don't want to have the burden of expectation laid on us. Are you less helpful than you might be to others, because you have been hiding from the spotlight? The good news for you is that you don't have to hide what you really believe about Christ any more. I think about a woman in that little church to which we moved years ago. The church was so poor that when they paid for the move, the check bounced. I remember how I felt going around my first week there trying to raise the money to pay the mover—it was really tough. I remember how badly we needed office equipment. They had a mimeograph machine that was so old it was like one of those things out of the "Adam's Family" TV program. It practically had a "hand" that came up when you turned the handle, and it reached out and grabbed the paper and pulled it through!

I went to the Administrative Board and said, "I have to have a mimeograph machine," and they said, "You just don't know how to work the one you've got." And I said, "Look, I have a Ph.D. in those things. I know how to run mimeograph machines. That one's worn out—Sherman brought it when he came to Savannah, and he bought it used." They put it to a vote, and they voted the new preacher down. They were not going to spend that money.

There was a little lady at that meeting who was the widow of a Methodist minister. She made about seventy-five dollars a month on her pension. She babysat for the rest of her living. And when that meeting was over, she quietly got up and went home with a resolution in her heart. The next day she got on the bus, went to downtown Savannah, and took out a note at the bank. She bought a new mimeograph

120

machine and had it delivered to the office. She came in to see me and said, "Pastor, here's the mimeograph machine, and if we need anything else, you let me know and I'll go get it." I tell you, the guys on that Board rued the day they ever let her do that! I hit them over the head so many times with that mimeograph machine, they would have bought a thousand of them if they could have gotten me to back off, but suddenly in her, the word *generosity* became flesh. It was no longer just an abstraction; here was someone who embodied it. I wasn't surprised when finally we built a new building there, and someone said, "What should we name it?" and they said, "Let's name it for Mrs. Cramer." She embraced something there; she made it real.

God needs people like you to make it real in every place you go. Do you remember the work, *The Great Hunger* by Johan Bojer? Do you remember the principal character, Peer Holm, who was a famous engineer? He had built bridges to span the mighty rivers. He had laid railroads across the desert—tunnels beneath the streams. He was gifted in so many areas. While still a rather young man, the situation reversed. He lost his health, and consequently, his standing. And he who'd appeared before kings and rulers was carried on a toboggan of ill fortune back to his old village to be a blacksmith's helper and to till the soil around that little town. People couldn't believe it—the great Peer Holm reduced to that.

If you remember his story, you know that he lived beside a neighbor who had a vicious dog. Peer Holm was afraid for his little girl, his only child. He said to that man, "Could you chain up your dog?" And the man said to Peer Holm, "Keep your mouth shut, pauper." One day, that which Peer Holm feared came to be a reality. He was coming back from the field, heard the scream of his little girl, ran and tore that vicious animal away from her throat, but it was too late. The life was gone from her little body. The sheriff shot the dog, and the villagers wanted to run that neighbor out of town, but they didn't. They just shunned him; they ostracized him. And in the spring when he plowed his field, they wouldn't sell him any seed. His field was left bare. The boys hooted at him on the street. One moonlit night, Peer Holm couldn't stand it any longer. He got up and took a half bushel of his own grain, and went over and sowed it in the field of his neighbor. You can't keep something like that secret. Later in the spring, the villagers saw a bare spot in Peer Holm's field, and they saw grain growing in his neighbor's field. They came to Peer Holm and said, "You, you of all people—why did you do it?" Peer Holm said, "I did it in order that God might exist in our community."

Peer Holm was no more perfect than you feel yourself to be. However, his influence in this most important way, helping others to become aware of God's reality in their lives, was very great. You may not have realized it yet, you may feel that you must leave this area to the "professionals," but you are called to this opportunity. In fact, your joy will become full as you begin to help others to know God better themselves.

You say, "This is not my style. I tend to avoid discussing religious beliefs with people. It's a personal matter for me." My friend, you are about to discover a completely new and wonderful experience. You can lead others, by the work of God's own power in your life and in theirs, to the greatest experience of joy they will ever have. You can help them spiritually. This is one of Christ's greatest works in your life; you can help others to love, to trust, and to serve him. You can introduce your friends to your Friend, and life will take on a new meaning for you.

# XI

# Hope Can Help

## *Overcoming Discouragement*

You might want to tell me at this point, "Look, it all sounds great. Frankly, however, I am too discouraged. I like the way it sounds, and I really would like to help other people. But with the concept of my helping them to grow *spiritually*, you've lost me. You are talking about somebody else. That is the last thing that I could do."

If you are feeling this way, I understand it. You are still discouraged about your own worth, and you do not believe that *you* would really be able to grow in this path.

This is where the gospel has more in it than you may have realized. The power of Christ is so great and so personal that even the problem of enduring discouragement can be overcome.

I want to give an illustration that may help to express the way you may feel when you are discouraged and there is little expectation or joy in your life.

In one of George Moore's novels, he wrote about the peasants in Ireland during a severe famine. Many of the people were given jobs building roads with primitive equipment. For a time, the people worked with their picks, shovels, and wheelbarrows. They

124

were so grateful to have employment, to have a reason to receive their bread, that they whistled and sang as they labored. After a time, however, they discovered that the roads they were building ended up in dreary bogs and swamps. In reality, the roads they were building led nowhere, and with that realization, a tremendous change came over the workers. Their cheerfulness disappeared. They became unhappy and disgruntled. They became difficult to deal with. All of their whistling and singing disappeared. The observation was made that, "Roads that lead to nowhere are hard to build."

If you cannot see light at the end of the tunnel, there is little wonder that your days are dreary, dark, and long, and that joy is conspicuous by its absence.

If you've read in Robert Scott's journal of his expedition to the South Pole, you know that in the opening part of that journal, the narrative literally sizzles with energy and enthusiasm. Indeed, the British had the colossal incentive of being the first nation, the first people, to plant a nation's flag at the South Pole. They were energized beyond belief by that prospect. However, when they arrived at the South Pole, they discovered that someone had preceded them; a flag had already been raised in that desolate place. The feeling of defeat in Scott's expedition became so heavy that as they retraced their steps, they began to faint, to fall, and finally to die.

Hope provides the energy that constantly replenishes, drives, and motivates our wills. Hope is the dynamo, and if that hope is removed, then we become very discouraged, indeed. It was a romanticist who sang, "When hope is gone we carried on." That isn't the way it works at all. When hope is really gone, you don't feel like carrying on. When hope is gone, when real hope is absent, you may exist, but life loses its boldness and courage.

In the novel, *Come Ninevah, Come Tyre,* by Allen Drury, some political leaders talk about the disintegration of America. They discuss our huge national debt, our seeming inability to pay it, and other problems, which are almost insurmountable. Suddenly, the Speaker of the House, an ex-president, says, "But there is always hope: We have to have hope." To which someone else responds, "Yes, but hope needs help."

Hope does need help. One way we become discouraged is by misplacing our hope—by placing it on the wrong thing. Certainly our hope needs help if it's been misplaced. We usually have some kinds of hopes, but our hopes have often been misplaced. We inadvertently misplace our hope by anchoring it to those things that are seen. That is misplaced hope. Real hope has to be based on more than the material. We need a focus for our hope that is deep enough for both the spiritual and material aspects of ourselves.

Now, I'm grateful that ours is a material religion. There is nothing in Christianity which says we have to divest ourselves of all material possessions. We don't have to be spiritualists and go live in caves without any of the abundant things the gospel talks about. We read those stories in the New Testament about the rich man, Dives, and about the farmer who tore down his barns to build larger barns, about whom Christ said, "You're a fool, man. You're going to lose your soul tonight." We read about those incidents and we remember that the principals in these stories were not condemned because they happened to be good farmers or because they had fertile ground. We remember that they were condemned because they had misplaced their priorities. They had forgotten

126

who the owner is. They had forgotten that they were called to be stewards. It wasn't the fact that they had material goods that brought condemnation. It was the lost perspective that blinded them to their neighbor's need and to the claim of God on their lives that brought judgment. They had misplaced their hope when they had focused it primarily on possessions.

Misplaced priorities and lost hopes always go together. The problem of Howard clearly demonstrates this. Howard had been a wealthy man. He had enjoyed the stature of prosperity and the community standing always given to a generous benefactor. Life had been good to Howard, now in his middle years, and he felt secure in the financial world his own creative, energetic hands had created.

Then, Howard's world began to crumble. First, there were several large investments that didn't pay off. Next came the loss of a substantial amount of money that had been lent to family members for a business venture that failed. Suddenly, there was a cash flow problem and Howard began to sell some of the land and other assets that had been a great source of pride for him.

When Howard's struggle became apparent to the community, the bankers became less friendly, more demanding in terms of their own protection. Howard collapsed with a severe coronary. He survived the heart attack, but his health was severely impaired. He felt unable to face the world without the security of a financial structure that was no more. Depression followed. Everything that had made his life secure and happy had somehow slipped away. Now he felt desolate and alone. His life was without meaning or purpose.

Howard had misplaced his hope. He had anchored

his life to the transitory, the temporary. The physical world had been so appealing and rewarding that he had become oblivious to the unseen world. He had, of course, lost his perspective. When he was stripped of his material possessions and then lost his health, his life lost its meaning and purpose.

Every time I think about lost perspectives, I think about something that happened to our organist at First Church, Houston. Scott Davis was in the sanctuary rather late one evening playing our great pipe organ, preparing for Sunday services. That particular evening, as he stopped playing to exchange pieces of music, he heard a bamming noise on the outside door. The noise was coming from the Main Street porch. One of the transients who sleeps on our porch during the summer months was beating on the outside door, saying, "Would you hold down the noise? We're trying to sleep out here!" When Scott told me about it, I thought, "That's the clearest case of the tail wagging the dog I've ever heard."

That's what the gospel tells us about hope. If we put our hope only on that which is seen and ignore the unseen, then it's like the tail wagging the dog and it isn't any wonder that we become depressed. We are brought low because we have misplaced our hope.

When Jesus gave his disciples power over the world, they exulted in that power. You will recall how they came back to Jesus declaring, "Lord, we healed diseases; we cast out demons; we were able to do all kinds of neat things. Lord, it's marvelous having all of this power." But Christ put their exuberance in perspective quickly by saying, "Nevertheless, let me remind you to rejoice most in the fact that your names are written in heaven. Don't ever get so blinded, so preoccupied with things of this world that you lose sight of the world which is to come." Now, that's the difference between real hope and hope that is not real. Real hope extends beyond that which is seen even into the world of the unseen.

Emil Brunner, in *Christianity and Civilization*, said this insight is precisely at the heart of many of our modern-day problems. He said, "We are so overwhelmed by our complicated problems and all that presses us on every side, that we begin to look on eternal life as though to believe in it is some kind of luxury." In reality, believing in eternal life is the only way to really attack our problems. It is the only way to come to terms with our problems. If someone doesn't believe in the eternal kingdom, then they are always trying to make a utopia out of this present world. After all, you only go around once, you reason. Grab all you can get on the first time through. People begin to experience a kind of time-panic. Life becomes a selfish cycle of grabbing what you can get and pressing on toward some kind of utopia where you will finally have it made.

Persons in the grips of that kind of hope vacillate between illusion and despair. They create their own illusions, believing that one more acquisition, one more experience, one more thrill will make their lives complete. And then, they get at least a portion of their utopia and they discover that the deeper reaches of their souls remain untouched, unsatisfied. They still don't have that which they need most and so they fall into despair.

This vacillation between illusion and despair is the condition that psychiatrists call manic-depressive. We're up and we're down, and at the heart of it there is a lack of hope. The person who has real hope in the eternal kingdom, who knows there is another world coming, that person is the only one who can view this world through realistic eyes.

At one time, the church was criticized for its otherworld stance. It was said of preachers, "The only theme they ever preach is pie in the sky." The church became almost embarrassed, a little reluctant, to claim one of the major tenets of our faith, namely, a belief in the world to come. But now in these gray days when we find the scope of our problems emcompasses human survival itself, we find that our greatest need is to have a secure faith in the world to come. Only when you are securely grounded in the next world do you have the strength, the drive, and the tenacity to live faithfully and well in this world. Only then will you escape being constantly victimized by illusion and despair.

If you are confident that your citizenship is in heaven, you are under no illusions about this world and its limitations. You can live without lasting, disabling despair in this world. You understand that you are supported by his love, and you do not have to be victimized by extreme highs and lows. Indeed, real hope is the Christian's heritage. It is your right. Hope is the helmet of our salvation. We must claim that hope. It is your source of encouragement, and it will help you to deal more effectively with your discouragement.

When Jesus performed his first miracle, he was at a wedding feast in Cana of Galilee. You'll remember that the steward of that feast was embarrassed because he had run out of wine. There were no refreshments to serve his guests. Mary, the mother of Jesus, came to her son and explained the predicament. Somehow, she knew he had resources that could respond to the need. Jesus was reluctant to grant her request, but finally agreed to do so. He told the servants to fill the six jars with water, and miraculously, in the filling there was a transformation and the water turned to wine. We remember that as his first miracle. Then, there was an interesting occurrence. When the guests began to partake of the new wine, the steward said to the bridegroom, "Usually the host serves the best wine first, and then, after the palates are a little less sensitive, he brings out the poor wine. But, you have reversed all of that. You have saved the best wine until last."

Now, what does that mean for us? It means when we have this strong, everpresent relationship with Christ, we have a quality of eternal life now. We have a quality of existence in this world that extends into the next. We have an inborn optimism that with Christ the best is yet to be. "Thou hast kept the good wine until now" (II John 2:10, KJV). You can overcome despair, because the Spirit himself is the guarantee of our hope that the best is yet to be. When the Bible speaks about real hope, it tells about a hope that is buttressed by the presence of Christ in human lives. It is not talking about the heaven that is "out there" someday, nor is it talking primarily about the material or physical. It is actually talking about the power and presence of Christ.

Once, I went to see a lady, who, I could see, was ecstatic. I inquired, "Why are you so happy today?" She said, "I just discovered that I'm going to heaven." I replied, "That's marvelous. How do you know that?" She said, "I heard it on 'Hollywood Squares'!" Christ gives you much more certainty than that.

Real hope is a living conviction borne out by the presence of Christ. Do you remember Paul as we see that heritage of hope in his life? Do you remember how, when he was on his way to Rome, the ship on which he was traveling was caught in a dreadful storm off the coast of Crete? Remember how they were driven for days by the high winds? The clouds obscured the sun, and they couldn't tell whether it was night or day. The storm was so intense they threw their cargo and the ship's tackle overboard. The Bible says, "We gave way to it and were driven" (Acts 27:15, RSV). But, one day Paul came up on the deck of the ship and told the sailors to "eat and take courage." Maybe they would be shipwrecked, but it was going to be all right. "For," he said, "this very night there stood by me an angel of the God to whom I belong and whom I worship, and he said, 'Do not be afraid, Paul . . .' " (Acts 27:23-24, RSV).

Real hope comes with the very presence of God standing beside us, saying, "It's going to be all right. In spite of the storm, in spite of the shipwreck, it's going to be all right." Real hope saves us from being driven by the storm . . . drifting out of control. Hope is our heritage. You can receive this gift of hope and overcome discouragement.

I stood one day on the east side of the Nile River. I had learned that the plane, which was to take our group back to Cairo, was late, and so I stood on the Luxor side of the Nile and watched the sun setting over the Valley of the Kings. Those of you who know something about the history of Egypt know that many of the pharaohs were buried there. I watched the sun as it sank behind those hills, and I imagined how it might have been for the pharaohs. The day they ascended to the throne, they ordered workmen to carve a tomb for them in the Valley of the Kings. They created an underground palace with various symbols, maps, and directions that reinforced a nebulous hope that they might survive death.

Everything was still and quiet that afternoon as I watched the sun setting. In my imagination, I could almost hear the chisels as they chipped away at the rocks beneath those hills. I could almost hear the ring of the hammers, and I wondered what the pharaohs thought as they reigned in their palaces, while a few miles away the workmen were preparing their tombs. I could feel the panic rising in my throat as I felt what they must have felt.

But, as I watched, the evening came down and a single star arose in the gathering night, and with the rising of that star, I thought about the Star of Bethlehem, and I wanted to sing the doxology! Because of that star, there's hope for each of us to gain the deepest transformation of our lives. We can open our hearts to the ministry of Christ and say, "In peace that only thou canst give, with thee, O Master, let me live." He will hear you. If discouragement rises up sometimes to haunt you at this point in your walk with God, it can be overcome. It is at this point that Christ can actually intervene in your life and help you with your low moods. Look discouragement in the eye and call upon Christ to help you take the steps to reject it and move beyond it.

# XII

# The Prayer of Power

## *The Practice of Prayer*

She had been hit by the death of a family member and a very close friend. Neither of the deaths had been easy, and she was profoundly shaken by them. In addition, she and her husband of thirty-five years had drifted apart, and she discovered that he was having an affair with someone twenty years younger than she. She was filled with grief, but couldn't grieve. Her anger was overwhelming her, but she couldn't get it out, couldn't release or forgive. She said, "I need God. Only God can help me."

I suggested prayer as a way to relate to God. Although she had been a church member for many years, she said, "I do not know how to pray. I believe in God, but I have never known him personally. Will you help me pray?"

When you feel that you have done all that you can to restore hope in your life and to overcome discouragement, it is important that you begin to pray more regularly. There is the point where only God can help you, where Christ becomes a very personal presence for you through prayer.

One of the ways you can begin to pray is by observing the technique of those who have learned the art of praying effectively. The first chapter of the book of Acts describes the preliminaries leading up to the experience of Pentecost, which marks the beginning of the Christian church. We learn in that chapter that the early disciples were "devoted to prayer." Indeed, the Pentecost experience came about as the culmination of the prayer process. Those remarkable disciples prayed and waited. Then the Holy Spirit came with impressive power. When you examine the method of their prayers, you can begin to pray again.

The disciples had the strength, which comes from the conviction that when they prayed there was a meeting. They realized that someone else was "on the other end of the line." They were not just verbalizing their problems to themselves.

Someone has said, "Christianity can be defined in terms of a meeting." The underlying conviction is that there is a God who wants to have fellowship with his children. He has created us for fellowship, and given the least and smallest opportunity, he will reveal himself and his love to us.

When Jesus was baptized there was a voice from heaven saying, "This is my beloved son." The Cotton Patch Version of the Bible reads, "This is my boy, and I'm proud of him." Don't you like that? Jesus based the rest of his ministry on the premise that God in Heaven is always trying to split the sky to speak to his children. He wants to meet you. He wants to have fellowship with you. This is the reason for the promise in the Scriptures that "where two or three are gathered in his name," there is a meeting. God is always reaching out to you.

You cannot make God just an abstract thought. You cannot make God "the principle of good." Can you imagine praying to a principle? God is a person. However, I believe we make a mistake trying to imagine what God looks like. That's why he sent his son. We can all see Jesus in our minds. That's where you should start if you want to learn how to pray. Start by seeing Jesus. He is here already, reaching out to you. Have an image of him in your mind. Sit down in your chair in your breakfast room or in your bedroom and see him sitting in the chair opposite you. See him as he listens to all the needs in your life. Listen as he tells you what he would have you know. Try imaging Jesus, and out of this conviction about a meeting you will begin to develop a devotion toward prayer.

Moreover, the disciples' devotion to prayer came not just because they believed God met them. They were also convinced that he acted because of their prayers. After all, he came to that room and shook it. He shook the place where they were. Then he filled them with such power that they who had been afraid almost to breathe, hiding behind closed doors, now took to the streets proclaiming fearlessly the word of God through Jesus Christ. God meets us in our prayers and he acts.

I'm persuaded one of the reasons why we don't pray any more effectively is because somehow this naturalism of our time—this determinism—has persuaded us that prayer doesn't really make any difference. Have you ever concluded, "what is going to happen is going to happen anyway, so why should I pray?" It is very easy to get sidetracked by this idea. The result is that this misunderstanding of prayer reduces it to a kind of inner therapy.

I sympathize with that mother who learned that her daughter was about to take a course in physiology. The mother wrote the principal saying, "Dear Sir, I don't want my Mary to know no more about her insides!"

Inner therapy, knowing ourselves, is helpful. We need to know something about our "insides," if you please. However, this isn't the kind of prayer I see in the New Testament. The prayer I see in the New Testament is not only the searchlight of truth to reveal more about ourselves (that comes later as an additional effect) but is also communicating with the God who gives strength to act and who helps us do something. He helps us do something not only about our insides but about the situation and the circumstances in the world. The disciples were devoted to a concept of prayer in which God acts.

You cannot convince my youngest daughter that God doesn't act when we pray. She had an experience that dramatized his acting for her and dramatized it for all of us. This experience began some years ago when our Siamese cat, Gus, disappeared. We couldn't find him anywhere. He wasn't to be found in any of his favorite hideouts. When he didn't show up at mealtime we knew something was wrong! Panic spread throughout the family. We started searching the neighborhood. We called the neighbors. We called the radio station. We looked high and low and could not find Gus any place. That night it was hard to go to sleep. The children were crying. Cathy came down to our bedroom not once but time and again. Finally she came down and said, "Daddy, when I said my prayers I heard Gus cry. I heard him meow." I patiently explained to my young daughter what was happening.

I said, "Now, honey, you didn't really hear your cat, you just thought you did. You see, you want to hear him, so it's a kind of projection of your wishes." I talked about "wish projection." Isn't that what a lot of people have called prayer . . . a kind of wish

137

projection? I said, "That's what's happening to you. You didn't really hear anything. You just want to hear him so badly you're making yourself believe you heard him."

But she was adamant. She said, "I tell you, Daddy, I heard him!"

Well, it was late. I was tired. I was running out of patience. I said, "All right then. Go to bed and if you hear him, go get him."

A few minutes later she came walking down the stairs with Gus in her arms. She said, "Daddy, I prayed again, I heard him, I followed the sound and opened the dresser drawer, and there he was!" (Gus had gone to sleep inside and somebody had closed him up.) All that time that's where he had been. She looked at me with indignation on her face and said, "I told you I wasn't just wishing."

You couldn't persuade her that God just hears our prayers but doesn't do anything. However, perhaps you have been disappointed by the results of prayer. Sometimes, it is probably not as easy to believe that our God is someone who acts. It's difficult for us to accept that. In addition, we are all activists. When we say our prayers, we sometimes get in God's way because we want to answer them before giving him a chance. We don't wait for him at all. Jesus told the disciples, "You stay in Jerusalem and pray until God acts through the Holy Spirit, and then you go fulfill my mission."

I remember being reminded of God's unique part in answering prayer through a parishioner in one of my former churches. Our church was trying to build a family life center and had to start from scratch. After much agonizing in prayer, we decided to purchase some land and to move ahead. I was on the committee to help select the site, so we started riding and looking at nearby property. After the search began, one of my most unassuming members quietly walked up to me and said, "Could you come out to the house and visit with me one day?"

I said, "Sure thing, George, I'd like to do that, but I'm busy trying to get some land. I want you to pray with me about it. I'm trying to find some property."

We kept on looking and a few days later George said, "You still haven't come out to see me."

And I said, "No, but I'm going to get there; it's just that I'm so busy." I was desperately looking for some acreage.

Finally, George sent word saying, "Tell the pastor I want to give him the land if he can stop looking long enough to come get it."

I was so embarrassed! When I drove up to his house that day, he was standing in the yard waiting to meet me, and I don't think I needed to open the car door. I think I could have slid out of the crack. I felt so small. I was feverishly and desperately trying to take things into my own hands, and all the while God, through that generous man's heart, had worked to meet our need. The disciples knew when to wait, simply to let God do his thing. They were devoted to that kind of praying.

Then, they seemed to have had a specific time to pray. They had an appointed hour. They didn't just haphazardly join each other at the upper room. They had a stated time to pray. People have said to me, "I just pray when I need to pray." I pray then, too. Those are little SOS prayers. Those are panic prayers: "Lord, I need you right now on this examination. I need you on this sale or business deal. Grandmother's sick; Lord, I need you." It's almost as if we have glass across our knees and a sign that says, "Break this in the event of trouble."

I'm talking about a specific time to pray—a time when we come to God with our individual and collective needs whether we feel like it or not. It's our time to pray, and we're going to pray. I'm not talking about prayer as a way out, a way to get us off the hook. I'm talking about prayer as a way of life. We tend to treat prayer like it's something we use when everything else fails. I hear folk in the hospital say, "Well, all we can do now is pray. We've run out of everything; all we can do now is pray."

Or as someone said to me the other day, "I used to pray the astronauts up and down when they first started going into space.

"Now," she confessed, "I don't even think anything about it."

See how life gets so routine. When everything is going along pretty well, we leave God out of our lives. Consequently, we never have any power in our lives. When the problems and the difficulties come, we really and truly panic because we don't have the inner resources to meet those problems. The early disciples had a time to pray, like Jesus, who, before he started the day, spent some time alone with God. They had developed what you might call "a heart for God."

"And in the morning, a great while before day, he rose and went out to a lonely place, and there he prayed." He was not ready to face those disciples. He was not ready to face the crowds until he had time to pray. When did he pray? He prayed at the beginning of the day; he prayed at the end of the day. Sometimes he prayed all night. The lesson for us is that he had the discipline of a prayer time. He had a definite time to pray. In between, there was no doubt that he prayed short-sentence prayers. While we ought to pray them, such prayers aren't the extent of praying.

Indeed, the Bible says we should "pray without ceasing." I know that. But I know you can't pray all the time. People who have a definite time and who pray regularly seem to have come into a kind of posture of prayer. I don't know how to explain it. It's like a great athlete or a graceful dancer. They've practiced. They have such discipline in their lives that although they aren't always dancing, you can just see them walk and tell that their bodies are in great physical condition. So it is with prayer. You don't have to go around with your head bowed all the time and your eyes closed. However, people who pray regularly have an attitude or posture of prayer. You can see them wherever they are, in all kinds of different circumstances, and you know that these are persons of prayer, because it shows in the quality of their lives.

To pray with that kind of regularity and power, the disciples had to be very devoted. They had to have a time to pray, and they had to have a place of prayer. To have a place of prayer is so important. You say, "What do you mean, a place of prayer?" The Bible says that God's house shall be a house of prayer. First of all, the church is a place to pray. Someone is going to pray when you come to the church. There will be an opportunity for you to pray right there where you worship. One of the things I like about the Sunday night service at our church is the prayer time. I see people Sunday after Sunday who come to our chancel rail and pray. I notice some of them like to go to the same place, and I know that's a regular place for them. That's their prayer place. I know the pew can be just like that for a lot of people. It's easier for you to pray when you're in your place in the house of prayer. You

141

will discover that one of the primary functions of the sanctuary is to help you to pray.

Some time ago the *Charlotte Observer* told about a cab driver who had a strange experience one Christmas. One of his customers appeared to be a desperate man who asked the cabbie to take him to the corner of Providence and Queens Road and just stop the car. The man wanted just to sit there for a long time with the meter running. He didn't say anything; he just sat there staring. For several nights the man asked the taxi driver to take him to the same location and do the same thing. Finally, the cab driver began to notice a market and drugstore across the way, and he finally concluded that his customer was surveying these stores in order to pull off a big robbery. One night the cab driver said to the man in the back seat, "I need some cigarettes. I'll be right back." While he was in one of the stores, the driver called the police and explained the situation. They came in a hurry. When they asked the man in the cab why he sat night after night in that particular corner, the man pointed to a window of the Myers Park United Methodist Church, a gorgeous, beautifully backlighted stained glass window. He explained, "I never have had much religion. I don't even know how to pray. My wife is very sick, and the hospital tells me she's real bad. But then I found this window. Something about its light gives me strength and peace, and somehow looking at it, I have the words to pray."

Having a special place to pray has enabled many persons to find the words to pray. That discovery has worked miracles in the lives of people.

I know a lady who at one time had terrific financial problems, and problems with her children. She and her husband had five children. Four of them were married, but your problems don't just disappear because your children are grown. Indeed, in some ways the pain intensifies, because before, you could protect them, but now, they often suffer in their own created difficulties and you are helpless to shield them. To see your children suffer and be unable to alleviate the suffering is painful. She was caught up in that pain.

She was a teacher. All day long she taught and at night she graded papers. Her life was so demanding she felt herself drifting apart from her husband under the duress of her daily living. When she came to me, she said, "I don't think I can make it. I feel like I'm falling apart." We talked about prayer. To shorten this beautiful story, she finally set aside a little section of her backyard as her prayer place during the spring, summer, and fall. On the bad days it was a corner of her screen porch. But she set this place aside and made it her little shrine. She got up thirty minutes earlier than before, made herself a pot of coffee, and took fifteen minutes with her Bible, *The Upper Room*, and her little shrine. There she read her Bible and a devotional and she prayed.

Her financial problems didn't get better overnight. The tensions in her family continue to this day. But something happened to her. She found a new strength, a new joy, and a new optimism even in the middle of those difficulties. One day she looked at me with shining eyes and said, "Pastor, a lot of things haven't changed in my family, but I've changed and I know with God's help I can make it." I was looking at a miracle! She had made a time, and she had found a place to pray.

I am so blessed in what I have in my study. It is what the French call a *priedieu*, a prayer desk. It's made from a chancel rail in a previous church I served. When we renovated the church we took out the chancel rail, but we made prayer desks out of every bit of it. I have one of them in my study. At that rail all of our children were confirmed, so it's a very special prayer desk to me. It's the one I use for my daily prayers. Somehow when I touch that wood it's almost like I touch the wood of the cross. I can close my eyes and be at the foot of that cross. I've discovered something else about that place of prayer. When I'm far from home preaching in some distant city, when I'm tired and worn and fragile and feeling vulnerable, I can close my eyes and see my little prayer place—see myself there—and a new quality of peace comes into my life and a new measure of strength.

Do you have a prayer place? It doesn't have to be elaborate. Just a corner of your bedroom, a little place in the yard, just a little nook, maybe a sewing room. If you don't have a precious place of prayer, get one. Make a prayer time a priority in your life. In a few weeks, in a few months, you will be amazed and overjoyed at what God has done for you. He can help you maintain your footing even in the midst of life's struggles.

# XIII

## The God Who Leads Also Precedes

*He Is Going Before You*

Did you ever have one of those glorious days when you feel like you have the resilience and resourcefulness of a cat? No matter which way you fall, you feel as though you'll certainly land on your feet. I had just such a day once when I was flying home from the West Coast. I had finished my meeting earlier than anticipated and had gone to the airport a long time before my scheduled departure in the hope that perhaps I could be fortunate enough to get an earlier flight home. I was anticipating an all-day flight on that Saturday and not arriving home until late Saturday evening. But the thought of preaching three times the following day with little or no sleep drove me to seek an earlier flight.

When I approached the counter at the Oregon airport, I found, to my surprise, that a Georgia boy was working for the airline. I couldn't believe my good fortune! When I told him about my need to get home earlier, he went to work on his computer and, before long, he had a ticket for me with only one stop in St. Louis. I was so pleased that when our plane stopped in St. Louis, I got off for a few moments to call my wife and to let her know I would be home around midnight. She had some troubling words for me. She

145

said, "I hope you're carrying some cash. Your associate left your car in the wrong airport parking lot, the one closest to the terminal, and it will cost you a great deal to get out." My heart sank. I had about a dollar in my pocket. I knew no one would take my personal check at midnight in a huge airport. After a time, I started to look around at the passengers who were flying with me, and I spotted a gentleman with an especially kind face. There was a vacant seat beside him, and I walked over and struck up a conversation. I discovered that he was a Methodist pastor and that he had preached a revival meeting in the same church I was presently serving! Not long after the conversation began, gradually it shifted to airport parking lots, and how much it costs to get a car out. Finally, I raised the question: "Would you cash a check for me?" and he said, "I'd be glad to."

When I arrived at my destination, my suitcase was the first off the plane. "It figures," I thought to myself as I walked to the parking lot, paid the bill, and drove away toward home. "Hinson," I thought, "you can split the atom! You are so resourceful!"

A couple of hours after getting home, the telephone rang with that ominous sound it makes only in the dead of night. The voice on the other end of the line told me about some special friends whose marriage had been dissolved and about a family member who was having major surgery on Monday morning in a distant city. Suddenly, I, who had been feeling so firmly in control, on a deck with both feet solidly planted, found myself on a sloping deck in stormy sea.

In this final chapter, I want to help you to trust in God's providential care more strongly. As you face the possibilities of your walk with God in the future, the deck will sometimes slope for you. However, God is going before you. I am sure that you must feel that change comes with breathtaking rapidity today. Ours is a generation of high technology. It is the age of future shock. We have a throwaway culture. Not many of us put down roots. The mobility of our society adds to our uncertainty. Some of us don't even go to the trouble of trying to make friends, or to establish a church home, because we're anticipating another move in a rapid succession of moves. Every time we worship, we bring a thousand questions. What about my marriage? What about the children? What about their education? Will I be able to keep my job? Will I be secure in my retirement? And above all of these questions, the great inevitable question, what about death? We are on a giant conveyor belt moving us inexorably into the future, and we seem unable to slow it.

Milton was in his middle twenties and was dying of cancer. He had a beautiful wife and twin sons who were two years old. He was not a Christian. A nurse at the hospital told me that Milton wanted to see a pastor. When I entered the room and introduced myself, Milton cut right through the generalities and reached for some answers. His emaciated body was filled with pain, and a host of unanswered questions filled his soul: "What will happen to my family? (There was no estate.) How will my wife make it? What about my little boys?" And behind these and many other related questions, there was the big question for Milton: "What about death? What will happen to me when I die? Is there anything that will take away my fear of dying?"

Contrast Milton's difficult questions and all of the enormous change we encounter with a less hectic time in our lives, when our days were not so complicated. I can recall, in the rural setting in which I grew up, lying in an open field on a lazy summer afternoon trying to capture mosquito hawks. I would hold an old limb up ever so still in order to get one of the tiny insects to light on it. Then I would ever so slowly lower the limb until I could capture the mosquito hawk. With my prize securely in hand, I could terrorize my baby sister! The contrast between that kind of an afternoon and the kind I and millions of others often spend on a crowded freeway jammed with bumper-to-bumper traffic is enormous.

Matthew's story of the first Easter in 28:1-8 is helpful at this point. The message of the angel to the disciples was never more applicable than today. The angel said, "Don't be afraid; Jesus is going before you into Galilee." The good news for us is that the God who leads us also precedes us. No matter what the nature of our Galilee, if we have the eyes of faith, we will see our Lord there. He has preceded us into every place where we ourselves must go.

I understand that you may feel this resurrection faith, which transformed the early disciples, is rather elementary. However, for those who were the first witnesses to the open tomb, the resurrection was a mind-boggling fact. It was an astounding concept that this risen Christ was really present with the disciples wherever they were. He could come through closed doors. He could be with them in Jerusalem and also beside the Sea of Galilee. Finally, they began to understand what he had meant when he told them, "If I go away, I will come again." Moreover, he had told them that it was to their advantage that he go away. "For if I go away, I will send the Holy Comforter, and he will be with you forever." When the early disciples got hold of the resurrection faith, their fears melted away.

How do you think the Apostle Paul lived with his frustration? He had ever so carefully planned his missionary journey into Bithynia. He had prayed and made his arrangements, but then, just prior to the beginning of his journey, he heard the Spirit and "the Spirit suffereth him not" (Acts 16:7, KJV). In obedience, Paul waited and was given the vision of the man in Macedonia who said, "Come over to Macedonia and help us" (Acts 16:9, RSV). Because Paul followed that vision, the gospel was taken to the Western World. However, Christianity did not have a very auspicious beginning in Macedonia. Only a woman by the name of Lydia, to whom he had preached at the laundry place beside the river, responded. Immediately after Lydia's conversion, Paul was arrested, beaten, and then thrown into the dungeon.

The dungeon in which Paul was placed was more than likely only about twenty-five yards from the famous Roman road that runs from the sea through Philippi and on into the Western World. He would have been lying there on his bloody back in the mud, with his feet and hands in stocks, listening to the sounds of the passing chariots carrying the people he had come to preach to. How on earth could he sing praises to God at a time like that? Paul was persuaded that a long time before he arrived in Philippi, God had been there. He believed that he moved into a future kept by God and this made all of the difference for him.

Look at Simon Peter as he has his great vision on the roof of Simon the Tanner. Simon sees a great sheet let down with all kinds of animals on it. Then he hears a voice saying, "Rise, Peter; kill and eat." However, Simon declared, "No, Lord; for I have never eaten anything that is common or unclean." And God gave Simon a great lesson that day, for he declared, "What God has cleansed, you must not call common" (Acts 10:13-15, RSV). At the same time God was breaking Peter out of his provincialism, out of his prejudice, at that very moment, the ambassadors from the Gentile, Cornelius, were knocking on his door. They were there to ask him to come preach the gospel to the Gentiles. The God who had sent the vision had also sent the messengers, and everything worked perfectly, because the God who leads also precedes.

The French call it *déjà vu*, already seen. Have you ever had that mysterious kind of experience of seeing a place for the first time and yet being nagged by the thought that somehow you have been there before? I wonder if at least a portion of that emotion can't be traced to the certainty that our Best Friend has preceded us there. Somehow, when our Friend has gone before us, things aren't nearly so strange, not nearly so frightening.

When you finish reading this book, you can go forward into a new life with God. The key is that we need to reappropriate our Easter faith. We do not have a great high priest who is unable to sympathize with us in our dilemmas or our radical changes. We have someone who has experienced every feeling which we have had, and because he has, he can sympathize with us. "Be of good cheer," he told his disciples, "I have overcome the world" (John 16:33b, RSV).

Once while riding along the highway, I looked up at a cloud formation which looked like a box. The sun was directly behind the cloud, and as I saw its beams shining through that box, I thought, "That's the way I feel. I am absolutely boxed in." I was having one of those down days when I saw no way out of my feelings of depression and loneliness. For a time I was saddled with my self-pity, perhaps even enjoyed it for a time, but then I looked again, and the wind had shifted the clouds and one end had been blown out of the box. The sun was shining through the gap! "That's the way it is with God," I thought. "He goes right on punching holes in our clouds if we'll let him." We are never boxed in with our Father because wherever we are, he has been. Wherever we are going, he has gone. We stand in the tradition of the Hebrews who followed the cloud by day and the pillar of fire by night. The God who was with them was also out there in front leading them, preparing a way for them.

Most important lessons have to be relearned. My own soul sometimes resembles a sieve. When I think I have something nailed down, I suddenly find it loose again. Early in my Christian experience, I learned the truth about God's preceding us. There was, in the little community where we lived, a country store located at the crossroads. Snipesville, which probably had twenty-five people in its best years, was the name of the little community near our home, and it boasted only that single store. However, every farmer in the vicinity for miles around loved to congregate at that friendly place. Not only could you buy practically anything there, but there were all kinds of interesting things to do. The men played pinball and checkers, placed bets on whose drink bottle came from the most faraway place, and did all of those childish things grown men will sometimes do. The only problem related to the store and its many activities involved the churches. The store remained open on Sunday, and sometimes the number of men congregated there rivaled the number in the little community churches. Some of the church leaders had gone to the owner of the store and tried to persuade him to close during church. However, he had grown tired of their repeated requests and suggested that they keep their noses out of his affairs. He was not a churchgoing man, and he did not sympathize with the plight his open store presented to the churches.

One Saturday morning I awakened with the distinct feeling I should go talk to the man about closing his store. I had been thinking about it for several weeks, but finally on that morning, I found the courage to ask my mother what she thought about it. She encouraged me. I never shall forget how I approached the owner of that store and asked him if he would mind giving me a few moments to speak with him. He was at least forty years my senior, and he looked at me with kindness in his eyes, and said, "Of course. Let's go back into the feed room and talk." The feed room was the most private place in the store. I recall as I walked into that back room that I did not have the slightest idea what I could say to the man that would make any real difference. However, somehow, I found some words to say. I cannot recall what they were, but I remember what he said. That man said, "Bill, you don't know how much I appreciate your coming to see me today. I started thinking about closing my store several weeks ago, and this morning I didn't think I could stand it any longer. You bet I'll close my store. And it will stay closed on Sunday." He's an old man now, just about ready to go to heaven, but he is a deacon in his church, and he is a victorious Christian. For many years, as long as he owned the store, there was an old sign which read, "Closed on Sunday." The sign wasn't really needed, because everyone knew where that man could be found on Sunday morning.

As I drove back home that day, I cried. I wept because of my shame of being afraid. The God who had touched me had been working in the life of that storeowner, and he had brought us together, and it was perfect. The one who guides us also precedes us. He will not send us into any Galilee where he himself has not been.

When I was appointed as the pastor of the Wynnton United Methodist Church in Columbus, Georgia, I was filled with a great deal of apprehension. Wynnton was a downtown church and practically all of its members had to drive past a number of churches in order to worship there. Moreover, they had recently constructed a large educational building and there was a heavy debt. During the first week in our new appointment, I awakened one night unable to breathe. Somehow I managed to alert my wife, and she got me to the hospital. The physician they called to attend me was a member of my new congregation. He attempted to probe my stomach in an effort to determine the nature of my problem. He practically sprained his fingers in the process! The physician turned to a nurse and said, "This man's stomach is tied in knots. Let's give him a shot." I remained in the hospital for two or three days. The physician was kind enough to let me get hold of myself and was even generous enough to give my malady a scientific name. However, I knew that whatever else he called it, it really meant "scared spitless!"

Upon my dismissal from the hospital, I went straight to the church. I was determined to go to the altar in that sanctuary and to stay there until God set me free from my paralyzing fears. I was just about to go into the church when I turned, looked to the south across the parking lot and saw a beautiful rainbow. I have no idea how many other people saw that rainbow that day, but in a very real way, it was my rainbow. When I saw it, I remembered God's promise to Noah. "When I bring clouds over the earth and the bow is seen in the clouds, I will remember my covenant which is between me and you" (Gen. 9:14-15, RSV). I was reminded by that rainbow that God keeps his steadfast covenant forever. I left that parking lot with a new assurance that the God who had put me in that place had preceded me there. I went home and told my family it was going to be all right. I didn't know what would happen in that appointment, but I knew God was there long before we arrived.

The prophet Elisha's servant was frightened out of his wits one morning when he looked up at the hills surrounding the camp and saw the enemy, a host of the Syrian army. With panic in his voice, he called out to his master, "Alas, my master, what shall we do?" Elisha began to pray and his first prayer was that the Lord God of Hosts would open the eyes of his servant. When God honored that prayer, the servant saw what Elisha had already seen—that between the prophet and his enemy there was another army, the Lord's army! We may not always see his footprints, but he has gone before us into our every Galilee.

Several Christmases ago, my youngest child received a puppy for a gift. We gave her the opportunity to make her selection from a litter of tiny fluffy peekapoo puppies. She chose a little white one who wagged his tail vigorously. She decided to name him Happy because he had such a happy ending. With

Happy's arrival, it was my responsibility to build a house for him. I set myself to the task and was rather pleased with the finished product. The only problem with the house I constructed was that it was extremely large, and Happy was a very small dog. (Having grown up on a farm, I knew nothing about little dogs. We couldn't have any dogs that wouldn't point, tree, catch, or trail.) When Happy looked inside the cavernous house that I had built, it scared him to death and he wouldn't have any part of it. It was too dark, too huge, and absolutely foreboding. I forced him inside the house, but when I released him, he ran out. I put his feed and water inside the house, but he refused to go inside. Finally, I gave up in disgust and went into the house. By that time Cathy had dissolved into tears. She was frustrated because of her dad's impatience and her puppy's refusal to cooperate. I watched her, and she sat on the patio holding her puppy in her lap. Apparently she began to think about the situation, for after a time, she, who was very small at the time, got down on her hands and knees and crawled through the door of the huge doghouse. Once inside, she lay down on the floor. Then a strange thing happened to the puppy. When he saw Cathy go inside, he trotted right in there beside her and made it his home. Someone whom he loved and trusted had preceded him there, and because she did, all the dread had been taken out of his darkness and all the teeth had been removed from his terror.

Jesus said to his disciples, "Don't be afraid. I am going before you. And if I go before you, I will prepare a place for you that where I am there you may be also."

Like the author of Hebrews, we do not see everything under subjection—the world is full of apprehension and uncertainties. However, "Our eyes are upon Jesus, and he is the author and the *pioneer* of our faith." He is going before you into your every Galilee! Now place your trust completely in him, as you never have before, and go with him into a future that is kept by him. Follow Christ into the future and his presence will keep your steps steady.

# Conclusion

## *Solid Living in a Shattered World*

Some years ago a friend spoke with me about being a navigator on an air force plane. He had directed several flights skirting enemy territory, where the slightest deviation in direction would spell disaster. He indicated that the responsibility of directing the craft was easily fulfilled when the weather was clear and all of the instruments were functioning perfectly. Staying on the right course was very difficult, however, when the heavy clouds rolled in and the instruments by which he guided became shaky, erratic, and undependable.

Hostile nations sometimes station small boats along their coasts with jamming devices on board, my friend said. Such devices have the capacity to interfere with the instruments that a navigator uses to direct the flight of the plane. Indeed, under the influence of jamming signals, planes have been led into forbidden air space and shot out of the sky.

My friend says a navigator's nightmare is that dark stormy night when you can't see the shoreline and neither can you believe what the instruments you steer by are saying.

I asked the navigator what he did on such a night. He replied, "There is only one thing to do: when you cannot see the lights along the shore and you cannot trust the instruments, you direct the pilot to climb. You climb until you are above the clouds, where the stars are always shining. Then, you get a fix on the stars—determine your direction from dependable heavenly bodies—and you can fly straight to your destination!"

Many of the signposts along the way have been obliterated, or at best, obscured in our fast-changing world. Physical movement, emotional changes, the loss of something/someone precious to us, and the clouds roll in . . . suddenly, we cannot see the lights along the shore; we feel lost and without direction. Moreover, those instincts by which we have steered our lives have demonstrated their undependability. We've given it our best shot, but we don't have the necessary means to give meaning, purpose, and direction to our daily lives.

Everything I have said in the preceding pages comes down to this: we must center our lives on Christ, who is consistent in his caring. When the clouds roll in, when you recognize the insufficiency of your self-sufficiency, you must "get a fix on the stars." You must focus your life on him who is the one who can always be counted on.

Let Jesus be your Good Shepherd. Open your heart to him, invite him to come into your life, put yourself at his disposal, surrender to his will and purpose, and you will enjoy peace, joy, and power—even in our shattered world.